GOT'EM GOT'EM NEED'EM

A FAN'S GUIDE TO COLLECTING THE TOP 100 SPORTS CARDS OF ALL TIME

STEPHEN LAROCHE
JON WALDMAN

Published by ECW Press
2120 Queen Street East, Suite 200, Toronto, Ontario, Canada M4E 1E2
416-694-3348 / info@ecwpress.com

LIBRARY AND ARCHIVES CANADA CATALOGUING IN PUBLICATION

Waldman, Jon
Got 'em, got 'em, need 'em : a fan's guide to collecting the top 100
sports cards of all time / Jon Waldman and Stephen Laroche.

Includes index.
ISBN 978-1-55022-980-6
ALSO ISSUED AS: 978-1-55490-980-3 (PDF); 978-1-55490-971-1 (EPUB)

1. Sports cards—Collectors and collecting. 1. Laroche, Stephen 11. Title.
111. Title: Got them, got them, need them.

GV568.5.W35 2011   796.075   C2010-906838-6

Text and cover design: Cyanotype
Cover image: CSA Images/Printstock Collection/Getty Images
Printing: United Graphics   1   2   3   4   5

The publication of Got 'Em, Got 'Em, Need 'Em has been generously supported
by the Government of Ontario through Ontario Book Publishing Tax Credit,
by the OMDC Book Fund, an initiative of the Ontario Media Development
Corporation, and by the Government of Canada through the Canada Book Fund.

Canadä

PRINTED AND BOUND IN THE UNITED STATES

ECW PRESS
ecwpress.com

CONTENTS

ACKNOWLEDGMENTS
STEPHEN LAROCHE

STEPHEN DEDICATES THE BOOK TO . . .

My father, Gerald, who has consistently supported my love for this industry and taught me the importance of having dreams and finding a way to make them happen.

STEPHEN WOULD LIKE TO THANK . . .

My co-author, Jon, who has made this project a wonderful one to work on . . . My amazing wife, Michelle, and my step-daughter, Guenevere, who are incredibly tolerant of my hobby . . . My parents, Gerald and Dianne, along with the rest of my close family and friends for their continued support . . . My wonderful friends who have been made through this hobby such as Baron Bedesky, John Pichette, Doug McLatchy, Fabio Del Rio, Russ Cohen, Doug Cataldo, Steve Feldman, Ryan Rajmoolie and Tracy Hackler . . . Dr. Brian Price for taking a chance on me in 2004 and allowing me to utilize my creative energy to help design some amazing cards . . . The pioneers of this hobby like Jefferson Burdick and Sy Berger whose hard work and dedication continues to be appreciated to this day. ◀◀◀

ACKNOWLEDGMENTS
JON WALDMAN

JON DEDICATES THE BOOK TO . . .

My dad, Arthur, for all the Saturday trips to card stores and shows over the years. Those drives are some of the best memories of my life.

JON WANTS TO THANK . . .

My co-author, Stephen, for all the hard work on the book. It's been a decade in the making! . . . My wife, Elana, for all of her support and for feeding into my growing card collection . . . My parents, Denise and Arthur, and sister Mimi, in-laws Irene, David and Jesse, and the rest of my family and friends for so much support through book #2 . . . My buddies Michael, David and Blair for the fun times at shows and card shops as well as the entire Winnipeg collecting community . . . My co-workers and buddies in the hobby throughout the years, especially Russ, Doug, Paolo, Rob, Feldman, Jeff, Tracy, Dan, Ira, Jeff, Stephen, Jeremy, Chris H., Chris O., Chris C. (and any other Chrises I forgot), Baron, Brian, Richard, Clay, Scott, Fabio, Mark and Jake. ◀ ◀

FOREWORD
BY MARTY APPEL

WHEN I WORKED IN THE TRADING CARD industry in the '90s, the hot term during those collecting madness days was "chase card." It was a marketing term to indicate the special cards, like a Michael Jordan gold-plated, glossy chrome, limited edition, signed, with relic, alternate version, that people would chase to the ends of the earth knowing it would make them rich beyond their dreams.

The key word to me was dreams. We had chase cards when I was growing up in the '50s, too, except we didn't know the term, and we didn't think about getting rich. The chase cards of that era were cards of your favorite team or favorite player, or in some cases, the missing numbers you sought to complete a set.

Somehow, I don't think I was the only kid in New York who felt this.

To me, the ultimate chase card was Mickey Mantle. Except for his "All-Star cards" or cards on which he might be paired with someone else (like Willie Mays), or a team card in which his face was only 1/16", there was only one Mickey card each year, his regular Topps card — no frills, nothing different than anyone else, and no other manufacturer to compare it to. It really didn't matter if we liked the picture or the design, it was the Mick! I promise you, I can still remember, all these years later, where I stood when I opened a pack that had Mickey Mantle in it. On the sidewalk outside the playground in Queens. That moment of recognition when you smelled the gum, peeled back the wax, moved past Harry Chiti and Russ Kemmerer and Norm Larker, and there he was, like a movie star, the blond hair, the handsome face, the bulging muscles, the uniform worn perfectly, the cap sitting just right, those pinstripes so vivid — wow.

I even remember when one year his height went from 5'10" to six feet, and I kind of knew, even then, that he was probably still 5'10" but either the Yankees or Topps decided he was somehow more perfect as a six-footer.

Stats? I know fans today love their stats to really know how a player does, but to me, the only real stats are the columns Topps gave us, the ones Sy Berger deemed necessary when he created the first set on his kitchen table in 1951.

The relationship between boy and card was just as powerful as between boy and girl a few years later. But the cards came first.

Jon Waldman and Stephen Laroche have done us a service here by honing in on very special cards from over the years. The exact one that clings to your memory (in my case, the '56 Mantle) may not have made the list, but somehow, we "get it." We know how it must have felt for a seven-year-old in 1933 to get a Babe Ruth, or for a six-year-old in 1958 to get a Bobby Hull. My son got a Don Mattingly rookie card in 1984 and experienced the same thrill. The joy of fatherhood was never better captured than in seeing history repeat itself.

I once thought there was something very personal, very solitary about a boy and his collection. I didn't think it was a very social activity. Then I found others who coveted the cards, and we discovered trading and flipping, and suddenly, we were part of a social sub-culture. When we grew up, we bonded anew with the phenomena of card shows. Here we were, all grown, able to confess that yes, when we see a sports obituary, the bubblegum card on which the fellow appeared is what we think of first.

Thank you, Jon and Stephen for recognizing that. And you readers — it's okay to have fun with this. I know I did. ◀ ◀

Marty Appel is the author of 17 books including the New York Times *bestseller* Munson: The Life and Death of a Yankee Captain. *He headed public relations and served as television producer for the New York Yankees and was the PR director for Topps in the 1990s.*

THE MODERN HISTORY OF SPORTS CARDS

DECADES FROM NOW, THE SPORT COLLECTING world won't be what it is today, much like how today's version of the hobby is miles different from the landscape of the 1980s.

You remember that time, don't you? It was the other BCE — the Before Cash Era.

Yes, as innocent and naïve as it may sound, there was a period where cards weren't kept in plastic sleeves or glass cases. Kids actually used to play with cards: flipping them, writing on them or worse — putting tape on them, pinning them to walls or placing them in bicycle spokes.

Then the boom hit and all of a sudden (or not so all of a sudden when you consider how long pricing guides have been around) cards were no longer pretty pictures and statistics — they were as tangible as stocks that could be bought, sold and traded on floors across the country. The New York Stock Exchange was in homes and school gyms across North America and beyond.

Like on the stock exchange, companies started popping up almost overnight. What was once a stronghold dominated almost solely by Topps (and its Canadian cousin O-Pee-Chee) suddenly was a boom market. Donruss, Fleer and Score were already mature when Upper Deck, Pro Set, Classic Games and countless others began to appear on store shelves. Adding to the now loaded market were a bevy of new food premiums like McDonald's, Denny's and Kraft, and unlicensed cards like the infamous Broders.

Many of the newcomers to the hobby weren't collecting for the pure enjoyment of reading a card-back bio or saving their favorite players in a special case — they were investors who believed that a fresh rookie card (RC) of a hot prospect was like an IPO, destined to take off in value and become a college fund feeder for their kids.

But, as we all know, the market was just too big. The collectors began realizing that they could no longer have one of everything and either specialized or moved on as prices for packs and boxes increased, while the investors decided that there was another "next big thing" market or simply lost interest and soon began leaving the hobby, looking elsewhere for their investments.

Soon the boom was over. Over the next few years, many companies either closed down (Pro Set and many fly-by-night companies aimed at the draft market such as Signature Rookies) or were bought out (Leaf/Donruss, which had been a hobby institution for years, was purchased by Pinnacle Brands, formerly known as Score).

But as with every boom and bust, there was an echo effect. Though it hasn't and likely will never reach its peak level of popularity again, the hobby continues to be a multi-million dollar industry. Companies realized they needed to change their strategy since the days of a collector putting together the entire assortment of cards from one product were done, and the high-dollar pursuit cards were here to stay.

Soon, the valued rookie cards were more short-printed than ever before. Chase cards had longer odds and more prominently had serial numbering blatantly advertising their limited availability. Perhaps most importantly, there was more player involvement than ever.

Back when the hobby took off, companies began issuing authenticated autographs in packs. Several series would feature a signature from a star player — the Reggie Jacksons and Patrick Roys of the card world — but by the mid-1990s, the autograph appearances would skyrocket. Some sets, such as hockey's Be A Player, would include one autograph per pack. This would quickly become the norm, and each company seemingly had a set like this.

The autograph, however, soon had a new friend — game-used memorabilia cards. They started in auto racing sets and moved quickly over to the "big four" sports as companies acquired game-used equipment from pro athletes and teams and would embed swatches in their cards. Soon, every collector could potentially have a piece of Ken Griffey Jr.'s jersey. Companies would also look to the past, cutting up Babe Ruth bats and Magic Johnson sweaters. Ever wanted a piece of turf from an NFL field or a ticket stub from the Super Bowl? Yup, you could get those from packs as well, or at least a portion thereof.

The highlight soon became some unique swatches coming out of packs. Thanks to the use not only of jerseys but their crests, or patches as they're commonly called, some truly attractive pieces started appearing. This would translate well to bat barrels or league emblems, which became the Cadillacs of cards.

Soon, it seemed as though anything imaginable could be plucked from a card pack. A signature of a long-deceased icon like Knute Rockne was available, or the very printing plates used to create cards were soon found inside foil wrappers.

As these cards became more popular, pricing for packs began to, shall we say, vary. The highest grade of product soon would demand $50 or more for a single package and steadily increased to suggested retail prices well into the three-digit figures. Names like Exquisite, Sterling and Ultimate would become recognized as the upper echelon of collectablility.

All was not good for the hobby in this brave new world though. Pinnacle Brands closed up shop in 1998 and would become part of the Playoff franchise. Later, Pacific, which rose to prominence in the 1990s despite being in existence since the '70s, would be taken over by the new Donruss/Playoff Inc., which would end up being purchased by sticker magnate Panini. Upper Deck (UD) would purchase longtime rival Fleer, gain control of the O-Pee-Chee brand name and even make a bid to take over its biggest competitor — Topps.

Meanwhile, UD would gain exclusivity with the NHL and its players' association, which in part led to Pacific's afore-mentioned demise and nearly forced Dr. Brian Price and his company, In The Game Inc., out of the hockey market. Price and other companies would still produce cards of hockey's past, present and future stars, albeit without logos. This would begin a new era, leading eventually to the NBA going exclusively with Panini, Major League Baseball only licensing Topps, and other such contracts, essentially looping back to the '60s and '70s.

All the while, the industry continued to shrink as dealers continued to close up shop. What was almost a card store on every corner in the boom era would shrink to a dozen or fewer stores in some cities, and long-running trade shows would either close up or measurably shrink in size. Additionally, magazines and price guides dedicated to trading cards would also soon fold or reformat, lessening the public presence of the hobby.

While this happened though, a newer phenomenon was taking shape online. Message boards where collectors could buy, sell and trade their wares were becoming all the rage, while several former brick and mortar stores found new (and less expensive) homes online. Auction sites like eBay were soon joined by traditional houses like Leland's in a virtual craze.

The rise of third-party grading also gave investors a bigger bang for their hobby buck. A new segment of the market was created by sending in a card to an authenticator who would assign a grade based on the card's condition. Powerful players like PSA, BGS and SGC were respected for their attention to detail and consistency, but there were also fly-by-night outfits that were simply trying to cash in on a trend. Assigning value to high-grade versions of the hobby's greatest treasures appeals to many collectors, and it looks as if professional grading is a mainstay rather than a subsection of the hobby.

Through all of these transformations, one part of collecting has remained tried and true, as it will for decades to come — the industry's ability to adapt to its market. Whether it's two school kids swapping cards on the playground or the young-at-heart negotiating a trade over Facebook, the core of the industry remains the pursuit of enhancing a collection. Whether it's a player, team, set, insert, jersey or autograph, cards continue to be at the forefront of the memorabilia world. Other fads will come and go, but that humble piece of cardboard will always remain the simplest and most enjoyable souvenir in sport. ◀ ◀

COMPOSITION OF A LIST

IT'S TOUGH TO PUT PEN TO PAPER (or fingers to keyboard) and come up with a balanced, thoughtful "top" list of any sort — but crossing sporting lines and regional preferences makes the job almost impossible.

That's why coming up with our list of the top 100 sports cards of all time was so difficult. Inevitably, we'll get some criticism (something we certainly welcome), but to give you a bit of an idea of how the list was created, we'd like to explain our selection process.

The first, and perhaps hardest, thing we had to do was remove any personal biases. Sure, some were easy to omit (after all, while Corey Koskie and Ken Wregget are important parts of our own collections, they don't rank anywhere near a top 100 card), but others endured major debates. Even up until our self-imposed deadline we were still iffy on some cards.

The one caveat that we near-instantly agreed upon was that no one-of-ones could make the list. We thought long and hard about a couple exceptions (notably the Lord Stanley of Preston autos and the infamous Allen & Ginter Fidel Castro card), but in the end our determination was that they couldn't be on the list because of their extremely limited nature.

Second, in most scenarios a card had to not only have appeal within its sport, but had to transcend its home turf and be a card that a larger community would want. So in the future if or when you see individual sports books from us, you might not see all of the cards in a particular pursuit listed the same way they are here, because a particular football card may be coveted by the general card collecting community more than its own.

Third, we started the list by ranking baseball highest (due to its decorated and colorful past that far out-ranks any other sport) and hockey, basketball and football equally. As puck hounds, this was a bit difficult, because, as Canadians, our natural inclination was to include more hockey than other sports; yet we couldn't ignore that football has just as big a collecting community across North America as our unofficial national game.

We found, though, that basketball really had fallen off the grid, especially when it came to older cards. We're not going to argue that players like Oscar Robertson weren't important in their sport, but the appeal outside of hoops is limited, and even inside, historic cards don't get the attention that they do in baseball or other sports.

Finally, you may notice that some all-time greats in sports aren't on the list, like Muhammad Ali. Here's an interesting case — Ali certainly would be on the top 100 sports stars of all-time list (possibly even at #1), but he has yet to have a definitive card. Heck, he doesn't have a properly defined rookie card at this point. So while we hoped to put him on the list, there wasn't a card that garnered enough attention to be on here.

We also consulted with numerous experts in the hobby, and to them we offer our sincere thanks.

As we mentioned earlier, we certainly welcome all feedback on our list, so don't hesitate to drop us a note via email.

We hope you enjoy this book and look forward to hearing from everyone who reads it. ◀◀

Stephen Laroche (stephen_laroche@hotmail.com)
Jon Waldman (jonathanwaldman@hotmail.com)

THE LEXICON OF THE HOBBY

EVER WONDERED WHAT ALL THOSE hobby shop folk are talking about? Here are a few popular phrases from hobby lingo.

BUST/BREAK ▶ Opening a box or pack of cards. Though most collectors use traditional means to open said containers, some have resorted to other means, such as scissors or hunting knives. (Don't believe us? Check out box breaks on YouTube.)

GRADING ▶ An authoritative evaluation of the condition of a card. There are several companies that will grade cards, but over the years many have been found to give inaccurate grades or trim cards to give them a sharper look. If the grade's not from BGS (or their vintage subsidiary BVG), PSA or SGC, buyer beware!

HARD SIGNED ▶ An autographed card that has been directly signed by the player, rather than one that uses a sticker.

HIT ▶ Denotes a good card pulled from a pack. Usually, this refers to a rookie card, autographed card or memorabilia card, but can also apply to a card with a low print run.

HOT BOX ▶ Defined by a box that has good cards, the term originated in the '90s when a box of cards had more inserts than the stated odds. The term also applied to packs that a couple companies would do that only had insert cards. Today, a hot pack or box often refers to landing two or more elite players in one shot.

MEMORABILIA/GAME-USED CARD ▶ A card that has a swatch of game-used equipment embedded in it. This includes jerseys, bats, shoes, skates, hats, gloves and just about anything else that isn't a jock strap. At least, until some company decides to take that route . . .

MINT ▶ The basic word for a card in the best possible condition. Cards can go (well) below this condition, but going above gets tricky, since graders will often come up with their own terms, such as gem or pristine.

REPRINT ▶ A reproduction of a card previously produced, often several years prior. These cards are sometimes done by companies as tributes to their earlier sets, but more often are counterfeit cards produced by collectors. Some will put "reprint" on the card, but many don't.

SP ▶ Short or special print, referring to a card that has a lower production run than others in its sets. This is now done intentionally, but back in the day, it was completely based on how the cards were laid out on a printed sheet.

TOP LOADER ▶ Also known as a "hard plastic," these are the standard protective holders for cards. Collectors will usually put a valuable card first in a penny sleeve (a flimsy plastic encasing) then in the top loader. Up a couple levels are screw-downs or magnetic holders (heavier plastic casings held together with screws or magnets).

UNLICENSED ▶ Cards that feature team logos or player images without fees paid for the right to use them to either or all of the corresponding leagues, its players association or the individual athlete. These cards are illegal and should never be purchased. A fair warning — these cards have seen a resurgence in recent years.

VINTAGE ▶ Refers to older cards. Most commonly today, this refers to any cards produced before the "boom" era, which saddens this book's two authors greatly.

WHITE WHALE ▶ The card that eludes a collector, harkening back to the tale of Captain Ahab from Herman Melville's *Moby Dick*. Some collectors will go through a number of channels to try to find that card that will "complete" their collection (though usually they'll just move on to the next pursuit). ◀◀

THE GOD CARD
1909–11 T206 HONUS WAGNER

WAGNER, PITTSBURG

THIS IS IT . . . THE GOD CARD. THE SINGLE item that every card collector wants, but knows they'll never possess. Even to get a glimpse of it in person is enough for most collectors.

It's the Honus Wagner T206 card — the one piece that, more than any other, breaks the collectibles barrier and hits the mainstream.

The story behind it is the stuff of legends. Ask any collector and they can relay the tale to you like a preteen reciting the lyrics to the latest Justin Bieber hit. According to legend, Wagner, who had the foresight to believe that kids should not be smoking, did not want his image to entice younger folk to purchase packs. While that theory is mere speculation, only a few of his cards made it into the market, making his the most desirable of all cigarette cards. Ironically, Wagner can be seen on his 1949 Leaf card with a big hunk of chewing tobacco in his cheek!

Of course, this is only one explanation behind the scarcity of Wagner's card. Another theory that has been retold countless times is . . . let's just say less altruistic. As documented by Baseball Almanac, "The more cynical view is that Wagner's public disdain for tobacco consumption was merely a cover for his anger at not receiving compensation for the use of his image to promote cigarettes as a popular product. He was, after all, known to be a sharp business negotiator."

Curiously, perhaps, it is one brand advertised on the back of the card that sticks out above all of the others on the famed Wagner. You see, there were several brands of cigarettes owned by the American Tobacco Company that issued the landmark series in 1909, such as Sweet Caporal, Polar Bear and a whole host of others. In fact, Ty Cobb, the antithesis of Wagner, had his own cigarette brand (and you thought Nike Air Jordans were the first product named for a player . . .). Each brand had its own advertisement on the reverse of the card, leaving the front to appear the same throughout the run.

Wagner appeared with two ad backs — Sweet Caporal and Piedmont. According to the description from a 2008 Robert Edwards Auction in which a Wagner with a grade of 1 was up for bids, the Sweet Caporal has been more plentiful of the two. Additionally, the Piedmont version is the card that seems to have captured the most attention, thanks in part to its famous one-time owners.

Back in the boom era, when baseball cards were *the* collectible, a collector who no one expected to step up to the plate made what was then a record-setting purchase — a man who himself is the subject of collector desire — Wayne Gretzky. Gretzky, along with then–Los Angeles Kings owner Bruce McNall and actor John Candy, purchased a beautiful version of the card for $451,000.

The mystique and controversy surrounding the Wagner has been covered in Michael O'Keeffe and Teri Thompson's excellent book *The Card* and the authors asserted that this famous piece of cardboard had been cut from a strip and altered by a prominent collector before being sold.

After McNall began to experience financial and legal troubles, the card was sold to Treat Entertainment to be given away through a Walmart promotion, and it has subsequently been sold at auction three times. In 2007, it was sold to a then anonymous buyer by Mike Gidwitz for well over $2 million. A 2010 *New York Daily News* article confirmed that the card now belongs to E.G. (Ken) Kendrick, managing general partner of the Arizona Diamondbacks.

In the years following the release of T206, collectors have had the opportunity to purchase Wagner cards from more kid-friendly products. He was featured in the popular Cracker Jack set just a couple years later, in its inaugural release in 1914. It's safe to say that this release was more plentiful than the T206 and it remains so today, though the condition in most cases is far from immaculate.

The Cracker Jack card isn't the only Wagner that came on the market after the T206. Around the same time as the famous set was released, other Wagners hit the market, including issues from Standard Caramel (1910), Close Candy (1911), Weil Baking Co. (1917) and a host of others during the premium era.

A few years later, Wagner would be featured in sets from Bazooka, Fleer, SCFS and others before the boom era, which propelled the value of the T206 to unimaginable heights. The card's popularity can also be seen in its numerous reproductions, including the 1995 edition inserted into Best minor league blister packs. Topps, who would later produce T206 tribute sets in the 2000s, also recreated the famous Wagner. Both copies have attained reasonable success in the secondary market.

The Wagner is clearly too rare a specimen for most collectors to attain (that is, unless you have at least six figures burning a hole in your wallet). Sure, other cards on the list are hard to get, but they are still within reach. Because of this, the T206 Honus Wagner gets its own special and well-deserved designation. ◄ ◄

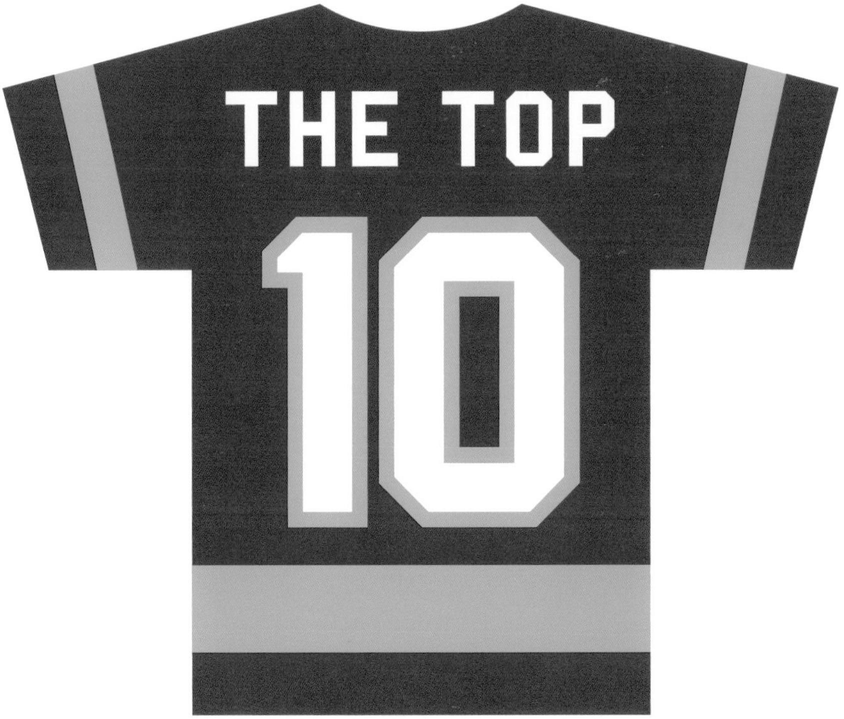
THE TOP
10

MICKEY MANTLE

Mickey Mantle

IF THERE'S ANY ONE CARD that serious, and we mean really serious, baseball fans will say that they need to have, it's this one. Considered to be *the* card of the last half of the 20th century and up to the present day, Mantle's picture card was from the last series issued in 1952, and it was a release where boxes, if not cases, of the card never saw the light of day. As the story goes, Topps had overproduced the final series of cards, even though it was an era when baseball cards would fly off shelves in corner stores. As a result, case upon case was left in the Topps warehouse, sealed off from the hands of eager children. Eventually, after years of sitting dormant, the cards were loaded onto a boat, brought out to the Atlantic Ocean and unceremoniously dumped into the depths. Mothers everywhere now had a model for disposing their sons' junk.

It's hard to say whether the card would be as desirable as it is if the available supply were as large as it could have been. An added, say, 1,000 cards might have meant much less demand.

But then again, probably not.

The popularity of the Mantle, in reality, doesn't have a heck of a lot to do with its scarcity. You can pick up an off-condition example if you're willing to pay the right price. Yes, you'll pay five figures, but it's not a scarce card, and surely not any scarcer than any card of the era that was seemingly destined for a scrapbook, bedroom wall or the worst fate any of today's collectors could ever imagine — bike spokes.

In fact, it's probably in greater supply than most cards of its time, because despite likely being thrown away in large numbers like so many others in its era, there was also a great potential that, because of Mantle's stature in the sport of baseball, more of his cards were kept. Sure, they may have been beaten up, but this was Mickey Mantle — one of the greatest players of his era who in 1951 was already showing flashes of brilliance that would make him a demi-god to so many. By season's end of 1952, Mantle was already a two-time World Series champion and an MLB All-Star game participant.

So what, then, is the reason for its popularity? Joe Orlando, president of Professional Sports Authenticator, a leading grading service, sees two factors in the popularity, the first having to do with it being the first major set that Topps, baseball's longest-serving and most popular card company, ever issued. "Even though Topps had a previous release [the 1951 Red Backs and Blue Backs], this was their first full-fledged release that captured many of the players in Major League Baseball. Most people consider this the first major Topps set," he said.

The second reason, you ask? Well, in this case, size does matter, when compared to Mantle's rookie card. "[Collectors] really like the larger format," Orlando remarked. "The '51 Bowmans are obviously a lot smaller and a lot of people really enjoy that really big, colorful format that Topps used."

As a result of these two factors, the '52 Topps Mantle has become as iconic as the T206 Honus Wagner. "There's something about that image that when you see it, it's just symbolic of the entire hobby," Orlando commented. "There's something about it that when you see it, you think about card collecting."

Of course, Mantle's career had an effect on the card as well. Had The Mick fizzled out after his first couple seasons, the card would not be where it is today. But Mantle would, as most of us already know, go on to have a Hall of Fame career that encapsulated three American League MVP awards, seven World Series rings, a rare Triple Crown award, 16 All-Star selections and a Gold Glove. He was also named to MLB's All-Century Team.

That's not to say, though, that the '51 Bowman Mantle — the rookie card — is any sort of slouch. In fact, that set was as much a landmark series for the company as the '52 series was for Topps, in that it was the first card for players like Mantle and Mays. The set offered collectors some beautiful art renderings and, in comparison to older series, really stands out in overall aesthetics.

Interestingly, the Mantle and Mays would be reprinted years later. In 1989, Topps, despite not yet going into full-out reprint mode itself (occasionally issuing "Turn Back the Clock" cards as a subset in its regular baseball series and highlighting former greats through promotions in stores like Kmart), inserted a throwback image into each pack of the 1989 Bowman set, the year the former brand was resurrected. Among those issued was the '51 card, both in a regular and a special Tiffany version.

Since the '52 Mantle was first issued all those years ago, collectors have had numerous opportunities to purchase authorized reprints of the original card, the first of which was issued in 1983. Later on, as the retro trend picked up steam and more legendary figures were included in series, Topps established an exclusive contract to produce Mantle cards. As a result of a partnership between the company and The Mick's estate, a variety of cards were developed, including cards that highlighted the pieces released during the Yankee legend's illustrious career. Most popular, of course, are the '52 reprints, but others, including those that incorporate newer designs, continue to be among the most popular cards to hit the market year-in and year-out.

With the great attention paid to the '52 Topps card, it was inevitable that seedy-minded individuals would take advantage of the card's lack of security and begin making counterfeit reproductions. As a result, collectors are warned to only purchase copies of the Mantle that have been graded by a reputable company.

The 1952 Topps Mickey Mantle has reached a level of popularity that few cards have ever achieved. Because of this, it is at the top of our list of the greatest cards of all time, just as it appears on so many other lists. With the card and the baseball hero's legacy living on, it will remain at its lofty position for decades to come. ◀◀

IF THERE WAS EVER A PERFECT trading card, it might just be this one — the Michael Jordan "rookie card."

Before discussing the card itself, and its depicted superstar, it's important to note those quotations around the all too familiar term. You see, the RC designation regularly denotes the first card of a player that has licensing by his or her league and/or players association. Other rules surrounding an RC have either been bent or broken, depending on the collecting personality you speak to, but the steadfast rule has always been that there must be endorsement by organizing bodies.

So why then is the Fleer card followed by the same kind of asterisk as, say, Barry Bonds' home run record? Well, because the Jordan in question was not his first-ever licensed card.

Set your wayback machine a couple notches and you'll see that for the 1984–85 season there were a few Jordan cards that were openly available in the market — those made by the Star Company. Several cards were issued that year of Jordan, including a base card and a couple subsets (among them an Olympic team card). All had the NBA licensing, so by that count the cards were considered kosher.

So why did the Star cards not appease the collecting gods? They were a legitimate company that had organized checklists and normal distrib—

Oh right, that's why.

You see, Star cards were not issued nationwide. Instead, they were limited to either team-specific or region-specific areas. This was a major problem for the powers that be in the hobby media who ultimately became responsible for making judgment calls about whether or not new criteria needed to be put in place. In this case, the question became accessibility — that little Jimmy Collector couldn't walk down to the corner store and pick up the coveted Star set that contained Air Jordan's card.

So, the 1984–85 Star cards, as well as their 1985–86 brethren, were fated not to be rookies, which meant that Fleer was in for a boom when it broke into the NBA market in 1986–87. Sure, other roundball luminaries like Charles Barkley had rookie cards in the set, but make no mistake about it — Jordan was and is the draw.

Jordan at this point was already turning into the superstar that many expected him to become. He had captured Rookie of the Year honors, played in an All-Star game and, despite missing most of his sophomore season, put on a performance for the ages in a playoff game, netting 63 points against the Boston Celtics, still an NBA record.

So even in this pre-boom era, when cards were routinely used rather than preserved, the Jordan somehow stuck out. Perhaps it was because like many posters of the era, the photograph captures Jordan in his classic slam dunk pose — soaring high above the rim, tongue wagging out, eyes focused on pushing the ball through the basket.

Graded or not, the Jordan card has become *the* basketball card to own. Through six NBA championships, numerous records and individual honors, three retirements (a record that will inevitably be broken by Brett Favre), one team ownership, a failed baseball career, gambling woes, marriage controversy and countless other headline-makers, the Jordan rookie card has endured and has maintained a standing of four figures in raw value. Finding a card that grades high by a professional service can push that card up into the five figures.

The magic captured on the card is one of only a select few Fleer cards that collectors have marked as "must-haves" in their collection. The company, which famously struggled to get into baseball's card market for decades, had a strong overall popularity that carried it strongly through the 1980s and 1990s, thanks especially to its Update series that nabbed baseball rookies early and brands like Fleer Ultra, Flair, Authentix and Showcase.

After roughly 120 years of creating confectioneries, cards and collectibles, Fleer was forced to file for bankruptcy in July 2005. The brand name would eventually be bought by the Upper Deck Company, who continue to produce Fleer cards in its sports series.

Perhaps this was fate working its magic. For years, Jordan had been a spokesperson for Upper Deck, and after his retirement (the permanent one) he was exclusive to the Carlsbad, California, company and was regularly being featured in products with memorabilia and autographed cards. Once the Fleer brand was acquired by Upper Deck, the opportunity to recreate the original Fleer magic with MJ was too much to pass up, and Upper Deck purchased several RCs, this time re-issuing them with Jordan's signature attached.

If there was any card that could rival the original, it was the extremely limited autograph that UD produced, but even that card's most popular day, the original Fleer card of Michael Jordan still stands as the number one basketball card of all time. ◀◀

The hunt for the next Michael Jordan starts here — in sealed packages of basketball cards.

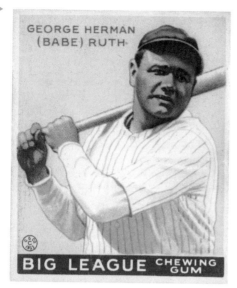

GEORGE HERMAN
(BABE) RUTH·

BIG LEAGUE CHEWING GUM

DESPITE THE LEGION OF PLAY-ers that have come along in the 60 or so years since he passed away, no one has been able to wrest the title of the greatest baseball player of all time away from George Herman Ruth.

Nicknamed and forever known as "The Babe," Ruth was the very embodiment of what any ballclub owner would want in their marquee name — a power hitter that was a home run threat each and every time he walked up to the plate, a star attraction who transcended the game and drew people from all walks of life, and someone who was so fan friendly that he would even stop his car in the middle of a street to sign balls for kids.

Ruth's marketability was never in doubt. His larger than life persona, which included indulgences in food, liquor, smokes and just about anything else imaginable, meant that he was likely to not only lend his name to a product, but genuinely like it as well. As a result, he became one of the biggest targets for companies looking for superstar endorsements, including Fro-joy Ice Cream, Red Rock Cola, Pinch-Hit Tobacco, Esso and Sinclair Oil, Old Gold Cigarettes and countless others.

Throughout his career, Ruth would appear on a wide variety of cards, including tobacco cards both domestically and abroad, periodical bonuses (such as the 1914 Baltimore Press and 1916 Sporting News issues, both of which have their backers as being Babe's rookie card) and others.

But it's the 1933 series by Goudey that truly won fans over as the most popular Ruth card of all time.

Or should we say cards?

GEORGE HERMAN (BABE) RUTH

BIG LEAGUE CHEWING GUM

For an unknown reason (though likely attributable to his insane popularity, even in the waning years of his career), Ruth was featured four times in the inaugural Big League Chewing Gum series. Though three of the four cards feature the same picture (two even have the exact same zoom-in, just with different color backgrounds), the lack of variety didn't mean that collectors appreciated the cards any less. Each one, in fact, is iconic in its own respect, though in many collecting circles it is the card with the yellow background that makes the cut as the most popular.

"I think there's something that's so classic about that shot of him," Joe Orlando, president of Professional Sports Authenticators, remarked. "People just seem to like that pose with that color combination, versus some of the others, even though the other three are great in that set."

The art reproduction, as Orlando points out, is actually of a photo taken by Charles M. Conlon, one of the most famous photographers in the history of baseball. In May 27, 1937, Conlon produced an article for the *Sporting News*, in which, among other subjects, he shared his thoughts about photographing baseball's superstars, and his comments about shooting the Babe make these cards even more remarkable.

"Ruth was easy to picture, and yet sometimes very hard," Conlon penned. "Most batters have a certain arc through which they swing, and you can set yourself for them. But you couldn't rely on the Babe swinging according to Hoyle. Most of the pictures we took of Ruth turned out to be excellent rear views."

Conlon, whose photos were impressively immortalized in a set of their own in the early 1990s, is most famous for his Ty Cobb sliding picture that captures Cobb sending third baseman

Jimmy Austin scrambling to avoid the Detroit legend's often malicious attacks to reach base and injure his opponent. Fittingly, Conlon bridged Cobb and Ruth, who were always compared and had an intense rivalry in their careers. In the same article, Conlon declared his player preference, choosing the Tiger over the Yankee.

"Ruth was a grand guy, always obliging. But strictly a specialist in the home run," Conlon wrote. "Not a Cobb all around."

Though no one will doubt Conlon's expertise in baseball analysis, there are many who would argue that, indeed, Ruth was the better of the two and the best ball player of all time, despite many of his records being broken, including the cherished all-time home run mark.

In comparing Hank Aaron's numbers to those of Ruth's, Orlando points out that there are a couple factors that, in his mind, place Ruth ahead of Aaron, regardless of the number produced: "It was just longevity and consistency that enabled

Aaron to beat Ruth; this is a guy [Ruth] who out-homered entire teams by himself. Put it in context of how far ahead of Ruth's competitors he was."

Ruth's legacy lives on today not only through these hard-to-find Goudey cards but through a multitude of recent releases that have paid tribute to the Babe. Companies such as Upper

Deck, Fleer, Topps, Swell and countless others have issued cards depicting Ruth hundreds of times over, while other collectibles, such as figurines and prints, continue to be issued depicting the legendary Yankee. But the groundswell of this memorabilia has done nothing to slow down the insatiable hunger that collectors have for Babe Ruth, and it's a sure thing that his legacy will live on for centuries to come. ◀◀◀

OF ALL THE SETS CREATED in the history of the hobby, none were designed quite like the Turkey Reds. Dubbed "cabinet" cards because of their size, these premiums are more works of art than simple trading cards. Using beautiful watercolor renderings to illustrate the depicted athletes and framed masterfully in silver-gray with a gold nameplate, these could very well have appeared in art galleries had they not been used as inserts in tobacco products.

Like many cards of the era, so many of the Turkey Reds are hard to find in decent shape, but not because they were dinged from being tossed around in unsafe packaging in a cigarette pack — rather, the packaging that the cards arrived in once redeemed wasn't exactly conducive to pristine conditions. Even the card's beauty worked against it by making it more likely to be displayed rather than properly preserved.

"The cabinets were mailed out to recipients in a rather flimsy envelope prone to being bent or folded," explained Craig Diamond, owner of T3TurkeyRed.com and one of the most extensive collections of Turkey Red cards. "A large number of cards were then displayed proudly with the help of pins, thumb-tacks or nails. Many also found their way into scrapbooks, secured by glue or tape. It's also common to find that collectors used the checklist back for that very purpose, marking a card as they built their set. A collector signature on the card is also not uncommon. Lastly, just the simple cabinet-size format lent itself to the cards being stained, creased or trimmed, corners being dinged, and all other manner of normal wear and tear."

Yet any collector who finds a piece in any sort of condition will undoubtedly pick it up for his or her permanent collection. The Turkey Red retention rate, Diamond comments, is pretty high, especially for the superstar players who invariably were more often sought out than the lesser names. The ordering process allowed collectors to choose their favorites, bypassing the mystery usually associated with card collecting.

Of all the baseball subjects in this set and of all the superstars that were heavily picked over, none compare with the Ty Cobb piece. Cobb, arguably the greatest base-stealer in the game and one of the most hard-nosed individuals you will ever hear about in all of sport, was one of baseball's greatest heroes at the time, standing tall as a member of the Detroit Tigers.

"The Ty Cobb Turkey Red has always been an icon in the hobby," Diamond said. "Certainly the set is filled with Hall of Famers, but Cobb rules supreme. The card itself is a glorious depiction and the extra care taken in its creation is evident in the detail of Cobb himself, the background and the majesty of the colors. It is simply a beautiful card."

Of course, a beautiful picture itself will only take a card's popularity so far. The appeal must also lie with the depicted player, and in this case, Cobb stands as one of baseball's all-time greatest players. The former all-time hit king won 12 batting titles and one MVP award during his illustrious career.

"Cobb was an absolute star at the time, on his way to becoming an original Cooperstown inductee and even now is considered by many fans as the greatest player of all time," Diamond commented.

It was an interesting dichotomy — Cobb was so well loved, yet he was not Mr. Congeniality. His rough on-field personality didn't make him a lot of friends on the diamond, with opponents or teammates, as was the case with Sam Crawford. Though the duo formed one of the most feared tandems in all of baseball during the Dead Ball era, they rarely spoke and certainly did not exchange pleasantries.

It wasn't until long after Cobb's retirement that his admiration for his teammate shone through, as Cobb helped rally to get Crawford into baseball's Hall of Fame. Cobb himself had entered years prior in the first-ever class, receiving more votes than any other entrant, including longtime rival Babe Ruth.

The fire ignited for years by the cabinet art pieces would eventually cool to a flicker as collectors' eyes turned to the new sets coming out — first the cigarette series, then the bubblegum cards. Though it would be decades until the hobby boomed, many cards were well preserved, staying packed away.

Eventually, as card companies turned to the past for inspiration for modern products, Turkey Red would be reintroduced by the Topps Company in 2005, first in baseball and later in other sports, including WWE (with an insert set) and football (with a full-fledged set). The sets had all the Turkey Red trademarks, including beautiful art pieces of solo players and action renderings.

Diamond was thrilled with the renewal of the brand, in part because of a special part of Topps's plans for the release. "I was happy to see Topps recognize the set. Topps was also able to insert several original Turkey Reds into boxes during the promotion. One can only imagine the thrill of seeing and receiving an authentic Turkey Red cabinet for the first time," he said.

No doubt, collectors will still get that thrill for years to come, especially as they try to track down this card. ◄◄◄

Some things never change: baseball cards still drive the industry.

Ken Griffey Jr.

THOUGH IT DOES NOT RANK as the number one card on our list, it's arguable that the 1989 Upper Deck Ken Griffey Jr. is the most important card in all history.

The card itself isn't, by any stretch of the imagination, a rarity. Though production numbers weren't released, and one couldn't even imagine how many hundreds of thousands were actually produced, it's clear that anyone who was a serious or even mid-level baseball card collector in the 1990s had one, if not a dozen, copies of this card. The reason for its iconic status in the hobby is that it was the first truly pursued card of the boom era. Everyone *had* to have this card, the first of a player who was considered the next big thing in diamond ball. Kid Griff had all the tools to be baseball's ultimate player — great field ability, a natural sense at the plate and a very likable personality.

Griffey's career would, in many respects, live up to his hype. He was a veritable human highlight reel, with outstanding wall-climbing catches in the outfield and a unique home run swing that would be the calling card for Seattle Mariner moments for years. Before being slowed by injuries, and shoved out of the spotlight by fellow Grunge City giant Alex Rodriguez, Junior was baseball's uberstar.

Griffey also did something that many players of his era couldn't do — he remained clean. Mark McGwire, Barry Bonds, José Canseco, Roger Clemens and countless other superstars who drove sales in the early '90s were either accused of using, or found to have used, performance enhancers of one type or another. Griffey was one of the players whose reputation was never tarnished, and even as his career closed, he continued to be a shining example to players around him.

Early talk of Griffey usurping Hank Aaron as baseball's home run king, however, would not come to fruition. Slowed by injuries, Griffey's torrid streak toward longball immortality went from sure thing to could've been. Though he would surpass the 500 and 600 home run plateaus, Griffey would not reach the 700 club.

However, Junior would still become one of baseball's most decorated players. He was MVP in 1997, captured seven Silver Slugger and 10 Gold Glove awards, made 13 All-Star Game appearances and won its Home Run Derby three times. Griffey was also a marquee man for MLB, endorsing products and appearing on commercials and television shows, including a well-remembered episode of *The Simpsons*.

Perhaps his most important spokesman deal, however, was with Upper Deck. After helping bring UD to a level of hobby prominence that some say has yet to be surpassed, Kid Griff was justly rewarded by being featured on packaging and a commercial that aired in the early 1990s. Though the other companies would produce Griffey cards of all shapes, sizes and orientations, he was synonymous with UD through the better part of the '90s.

Through it all, the 1989 rookie has remained the iconic image of Griffey. Even today, the card, unlike many of its boom era brothers, has not lost its luster and collectability.

Few cards in history can lay claim to this level of fame, especially when the player they depict has had the rocky road that Griffey has traveled in the latter stages of his career. Like so many players who were sports idols in the early 1990s, fans and collectors alike have had to endure Griffey's descent into average-ness.

But as was the case with Don Mattingly, Wade Boggs and other superstars whose careers we watched decline over the years, Griffey's position as a hero in baseball remained intact despite those later years. Through trials and tribulations, Griffey would still pack stadiums with fans clamoring to see that unmistakable swing. He would also return to Seattle for his swan song, and though his spectacular wall-climbing days were long behind him, he could still draw fans like no other could in the city.

Curiously, as of 2009, Griffey had not been given what is perhaps Upper Deck's highest honor — the mini tribute of a Baseball Heroes insert. The series that included Reggie Jackson, Nolan Ryan and Ted Williams among others had, at the time of the hobby boom, been a prestigious series that recognized unparalleled excellence in sport before losing some of its luster in becoming a full set in 2005.

Undoubtedly, there are far greater honors that await Junior when he does retire. And when Griffey's Cooperstown bust is finished, don't be surprised if it is modeled after the smile on this card, by far the most collectible of one of baseball's all-time greats. ◀ ◀

Could a Griffey Jr. rookie be sitting in this pack?

1979-80 O-PEE-CHEE WAYNE GRETZKY

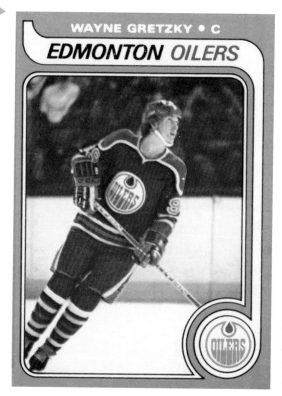

6

OVER THE COURSE OF 21 pro seasons, Wayne Gretzky revolutionized the game of hockey, and his rookie cards from the 1979–80 Topps and O-Pee-Chee releases have long been the most popular in the hobby.

Gretzky's legendary career began at the age of 17 as a member of the Indianapolis Racers of the World Hockey Association, when they signed him as an underage junior player. He would only last eight games with the club as their financial woes forced them to trade him to the Edmonton Oilers in a primarily cash deal on November 2, 1978. The Racers wouldn't last much longer, disbanding a little over a month later.

Steve Babineau is a Boston-based photographer who produced many of the images used in classic Topps and O-Pee-Chee hockey card sets in the 1970s and 1980s. A week after the trade, he traveled to Springfield, Massachusetts, where the New England Whalers were playing while the Hartford Civic Center was being repaired after its roof had blown off in a windstorm. "I was shooting the WHA for *The Hockey News* at the time, so it was important to be there for Gretzky's first game that I could get to," he said. "Unfortunately, I don't have the negative for this shot anymore as it was from one of the few seasons that Topps didn't return my shots to me."

At the end of the season, the WHA had finally ceased operations after seven incredible years where they proved to the NHL that they could compete. The senior loop would absorb four teams, including the Oilers, and Gretzky would remain property of the club heading into the 1979–80 campaign. As a result of the merger, Topps was able to include some of the former WHA stars in their new hockey card set, and it was only natural that the hottest young name in hockey would be a part of their collection.

Topps would usually produce their hockey card set first and would allow O-Pee-Chee to add more cards to the set or make changes for their Canadian release. Between the 1968–69 and 1991–92 seasons, both companies produced sets featuring the same design, but the O-Pee-Chee version traditionally is in higher demand since their set was printed on better card stock and featured a larger number of players.

The Gretzky rookie card found in O-Pee-Chee packs has two distinct variations that collectors can keep their eyes open for. In the earlier part of the print run, there are print lines that can be found trailing off the small cartoon on the back of the card. The entire series seems to have been produced in smaller quantities in comparison to those from the previous two seasons and there are some people who believe that a strike at the O-Pee-Chee factory may have caused this decreased number of cards available on the market.

Gretzky's first season in the NHL was one for the ages as he scored 51 goals and tied for the league's scoring lead with veteran Marcel Dionne of the Los Angeles Kings. As the 1980s continued, he began to rewrite the league's record book as he earned 109 assists in 1980–81 and scored 92 goals and racked up 212 points the year after. He later broke those single-season standards for assists and points. After four Stanley Cup titles with Edmonton, he was shockingly traded to the Los Angeles Kings on August 9, 1988, and he would become hockey's all-time scoring leader during the 1989–90 season when he surpassed his idol, the legendary Gordie Howe.

It was around that time when more people were paying attention to the investment potential of hockey cards and his

O-Pee-Chee card was regularly trading at $100 or more for copies in top condition. A year later, that same item had risen to over $700 in some areas as the supply simply could not keep up with demand. As more people stepped away from the hobby, this would change, but the card would stay at this approximate value for the rest of his career.

Another problem that rose with the popularity of the Gretzky rookie card was the appearance of counterfeit versions. It is fairly easy to detect a fake as the print dot on his shoulder does not show up, and there are other key indicators that allow one to be spotted. For the novice collector or one who is not totally familiar with the 1979–80 O-Pee-Chee release, the best route to take when purchasing this card is to grab a graded copy. ◀ ◀◀

Today, there are more than 5,000 different Wayne Gretzky cards available.

LARRY BIRD/JULIUS ERVING/MAGIC JOHNSON

7

TOPPS HAS always had a reputation of being experimental, but there were few things as puzzling, though ultimately endearing, as their 1980–81 basketball set. By taking a standard-sized card and dividing it into three smaller perforated cards, they were attempting to breathe life back into a sagging segment of the market and, in the process, created one of their greatest cards ever.

In 1979–80, the two hottest rookies in the NBA were Larry Bird of the Boston Celtics and Earvin "Magic" Johnson Jr. of the Los Angeles Lakers. Throughout the year, the pair would vie for the league's Rookie of the Year award, which was ultimately won by Bird. Johnson wouldn't go unrewarded, as he was named the Most Valuable Player of the NBA Finals that year after his club defeated Julius Erving and the Philadelphia 76ers.

All three of the players listed above were brought together on cardboard by Topps the following season, and whether or not the combination was intentional, one of the greatest basketball cards of all time had been created when the "regular" mini-cards of Johnson and Bird were combined with a Scoring Leader subset card of Erving. All three players had multiple cards in the set, and they appeared on a staggering number of combinations with other players.

As for the set itself, the design is a bit of a throwback to the Trios sticker set that appeared in packs of the 1971–72 product, but it also bears a striking resemblance to the 1978 baseball series.

To this day, the numbering for the set creates some confusion as there are 176 different mini-cards and 264 different larger cards. Essentially, each mini card appears three times, but as part of different combinations. It was a bold move, but it did little to turn basketball cards into a must-have item for kids.

Since the set itself was a major flop, Topps would only try to make basketball cards for one more season before giving them up until 1992–93. However, the much-maligned series would take on a new life in the boom years when overstocked wax packs were quickly scooped up by speculators trying to get their hands on this card, and prices seemed to rise on a regular basis. Helping this along were the amazing on-court performances of both Bird and Johnson, whose rivalry has gone down as one of the greatest in sports history. They would meet three times in the NBA Finals during the 1980s, and the animosity between fans in Los Angeles and Boston would help the game's popularity soar to great heights.

Today, the card hasn't lost much of its luster and is still considered a must-have for most vintage basketball card collectors. For those of us who grew up watching the epic struggle between the Celtics and the Lakers, this card acts as a reminder of the days when the NBA was growing by leaps and bounds and two of its young stars were ready to go down in history among the greatest of all time.

It is, of course, fitting that these two players would debut on the same card, as their battles on the court would become legendary and their careers would be forever linked. Like Sidney Crosby and Alexander Ovechkin in hockey, Johnson and Bird fueled the NBA in its rebuilding era. Hurting from low attendance and an extremely small presence on TV, hoops was ready for new superstars to hang its hat on. Two teams with young and exciting players was the cure for what ailed the NBA; the soft spoken Bird and flashy Johnson carried the league on its shoulders for years.

Of course, it certainly helped that the Lakers and Celtics were already two of the league's most storied franchises and had great supporting casts. Bird's group, which won championships in 1981, 1984 and 1986, also had the likes of Robert

Parish, while Johnson was seconded by James Worthy and other stars in a decade when the Lakers rang up five NBA titles (1980, 1982, 1985, 1987 and 1988). Johnson and Bird would also count six MVP titles between them (three each), be named to the All-NBA First Team nine times apiece, be named to the NBA's 50th Anniversary All-Time Team, team up to win the gold medal at the 1992 Summer Olympics and receive other accolades throughout their careers. Both men were also inducted into the NBA's Hall of Fame. ◀ ◀

Certified autographs are commonly placed on stickers before they are attached to a card. Imagine how many of these Bird, Dr. J and Magic would've signed had the trend started in the early 1980s.

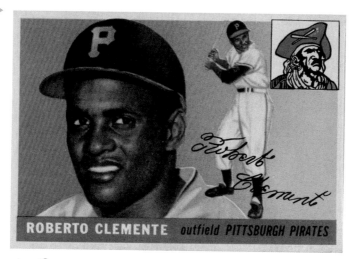

ROBERTO CLEMENTE *outfield* **PITTSBURGH PIRATES**

FEW PLAYERS have had as significant an impact on the game of baseball as Roberto Clemente, and his story continues to serve as an inspiration to millions of fans almost 40 years after his tragic and untimely death.

Born in Carolina, Puerto Rico, in 1934, Clemente became a local star as a teenager before joining the Santurce Crabbers club and being offered a contract by the Brooklyn Dodgers organization. He would head north to play for the Montreal Royals farm team, but the Pittsburgh Pirates would snag his rights during a rookie draft on November 22, 1954.

Clemente started the 1955 season on the Pirates' roster and made his debut, ironically, against Brooklyn. Despite some struggles due to racial tension, he would prove to be a solid acquisition and batted .255 as a rookie, also showing off some impressive defensive potential. It was at this time when Topps decided to take a chance and depict the young star in their annual baseball card set.

The 1955 collection is beloved by collectors due to its horizontal orientation and use of two player photos on a colorful background. Strangely, Bowman did not feel the need to sign him to a deal to be a part of their release that year, and they would be out of the game the following year.

Throughout the rest of the 1950s and into the 1960s, Clemente's star rose with each passing year. In 1960, he became an All-Star for the first time in his career and was a key part of Pittsburgh's World Series championship club. The following year was a big one as well since he led the National League with a .351 batting average and won his first of what eventually became 12 consecutive Gold Glove Awards.

The accolades kept coming for the right fielder as he would be named the National League's Most Valuable Player in 1966 with a career-best 29 home runs and 119 runs batted in. He would bat .300 in all but one season in the 1960s and he was a perennial All-Star whose fan base increased with each passing season. In 1970, the Pirates returned to postseason action but lost to the Cincinnati Reds in the National League Championship Series. A year later, they would defeat the Baltimore Orioles in a tight seven-game World Series, and Clemente was named the Most Valuable Player as he hit .414.

In 1972, Clemente would become a member of baseball's vaunted 3,000-hit club and the Pirates would make it to the playoffs for the third year in a row. On December 23 of that year, a massive earthquake hit Managua, Nicaragua, and he took it quite personally since he had been in the city just three weeks beforehand. He worked hard as part of the relief effort but found out that three planeloads of aid had been diverted by the Nicaraguan government. Believing that his presence on a flight might actually bring supplies to those affected by the earthquake, he boarded a plane on December 31, but it crashed off the coast of Isla Verde, Puerto Rico, shortly after takeoff. Fans everywhere went into mourning as baseball lost one of its most inspirational and beloved personalities.

Less than three months later, the Baseball Hall of Fame held a special election and Clemente was granted membership without the customary waiting period. Other posthumous accolades included a Congressional Gold Medal and the first Presidential Citizens Medal. Major League Baseball issues its Commissioner's Historic Achievement Award in Clemente's memory. It is given out each year to the player who best exemplifies the game of baseball, sportsmanship, community involvement and the individual's contribution to his team.

Though it's often been considered a touchy subject for collectors, some collectibles were issued following Clemente's passing as tribute pieces, such as the famed "Last Walk in Tunnel" photo of Clemente's approach to the diamond before what would be his final game. One of the most interesting items to surface was the "Roberto Clemente Memorial Album." Authorized by MLB and the Pittsburgh Pirates, the recording is available on tape or CD in Spanish or English and features interviews that cover highlights of Clemente's career. Interestingly, Clemente's last Topps card from his active career, the 1973 issue, does not mention his passing but does reflect his 3,000th hit.

Clemente's cards continue to be extremely popular today as fans of different generations are drawn to his story. The rookie card is certainly one of the most prized, in addition to authentic autographs and game-used memorabilia. It is unlikely that the demand for his cards will subside. In fact, it may yet intensify due to his status as one of the greatest legends and humanitarians in sporting history. ◀ ◀

Back in the day, that unmistakable piece of chewing gum was just as anticipated as the cards.

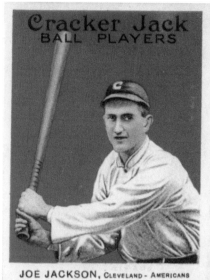

Cracker Jack
BALL PLAYERS

JOE JACKSON, Cleveland - Americans

THERE HAVE BEEN MANY BOOKS written about the greatest athletes in history. It's almost expected that when an athlete reaches a certain level of stardom (or at least a promise of stardom) that at least one biography, if not an autobiography, will be composed, and at times books will follow an athlete's passing to tell the full story of his or her life.

It's rare, however, for a real athlete to become part of fiction, but those who have become part of some of the most iconic books of all time. Of those books, it can easily be argued that none captured generations of sports fans like *Shoeless Joe*. Written by Canadian author W.P. Kinsella and later adapted into the Hollywood classic *Field of Dreams*, *Shoeless Joe* is a masterful book that relays the story of Jackson's spirit living on after the book's main character, Ray Kinsella, builds a baseball diamond in his Iowa cornfield.

Like many kids' understanding of athletes from days gone by, Kinsella's connection to Jackson came through his father: "My dad used to talk about Shoeless Joe, felt he had been badly treated. I loved the name, better than anything I could invent. I just said *what if* — which is what fiction writers spend their lives doing — Joe Jackson came back to life in this time and space, which was Iowa City, Iowa, 1978."

Kinsella's fascination with Jackson certainly wasn't unique. Before and long after the Black Sox controversy, Jackson was considered by most to be one of the greatest players in the era leading up and into World War I. A natural superstar, "Shoeless"

Joe, who earned his nickname by refusing to wear cleats during a minor league game because they had given him blisters one day earlier, was a one-time .400 hitter in the big leagues and was the centerpiece of the 1917 World Series victory by the Chicago White Sox.

Though his career stats are Hall of Fame–worthy, Shoeless Joe has been kept out of Cooperstown thanks to Kenesaw Mountain Landis, baseball's first commissioner, who banned Jackson from the game for life, along with seven other players from Chicago, all allegedly involved in the 1919 Black Sox scandal, in which the team was believed to have thrown the World Series to the Cincinnati Reds.

To this day, Jackson's legacy remains outside Cooperstown, but his memory lives on. Despite his rejection by the baseball establishment, fans still discuss him extensively. Though Kinsella admits his book has helped keep the legacy alive, he insists it's not solely responsible. "I think it has helped, but I think the legend would have continued and will continue until he gets into the Hall of Fame as he deserves," said the author.

Helping to keep Jackson's memory alive is a renewed devotion by card companies to Shoeless Joe, including a 1993 card produced by Cracker Jack. That card was one of 24 produced by the still popular confectionery company that paid homage to the 1915 series. And while the 1915 series has become one of the most desired in the history of baseball cards, its predecessor is the more highly coveted.

You see, back in 1914, cards produced for kids were a rare treat. More often, the popular cardboard pieces were found in packets of cigarettes, but Cracker Jack's producers Rueckheim Bros. & Eckstein, saw an opportunity to build their brand by including the popular stars of the era in its boxes of caramel-coated popcorn and peanuts. The company had already been including kid-friendly bonus prizes in its boxes for two years, when it chose to create its first baseball series.

Though the cards were issued in protective sleeves, they were still extremely susceptible to damage from the oil and salt that the snack was coated in. Add to this that kids likely would, at most, lick their fingers before retrieving their prize and you have the recipe for highly damaged cards.

The method for procuring 1915 cards, however, was quite different, as they could be redeemed by special mail-in offer to RB&E. The result is that the 1915 series, which included many of the same cards and images as the 1914 edition, is easier to find in better condition than the 1914s.

After those releases, Cracker Jack mysteriously stopped producing cards. It wasn't until the 1980s, in fact, that the next Cracker Jack series would be found in the confectionery treat. In the 1990s, Cracker Jack teamed first with the Topps Company (then Donruss Inc.) to produce miniature versions of the company's larger pack-issued sets, leading up to the 1993 reprint series. Following this, Cracker Jack would produce one more independent series in 1997 before fostering a solid relationship with Topps in 2002 and 2003 that saw a couple sets issued in the treat, as well as traditionally issued Topps series in 2004 and 2005.

Through all these incarnations, the 1914 "Shoeless" Joe Jackson card remains the most popular card in the history of Cracker Jack. ◄ ◄

Thousands of collectors visit national trading card shows every year.

1948-49 LEAF
JACKIE ROBINSON

JACKIE ROBINSON

SOMETIMES FOR A COLLECTOR the monetary value of a trading card will pale in comparison to the impact a player had on their sport and society. A perfect case for this notion is that of Jackie Robinson, who broke the color barrier in baseball and still serves as an inspiration to all.

In the 1940s, baseball, like all other major sports in the United States, experienced segregation between white athletes and those of color. Progressive thinkers at the time seriously began to question why the color barrier even existed and Brooklyn Dodgers President and General Manager Branch Rickey began to scout the Negro Leagues for a player, and he found Robinson, formerly a solid amateur athlete, playing for the Kansas City Monarchs. He sent the young star to play for Brooklyn's farm club in Montreal, and after a full season there, on April 15, 1947, Robinson became the first black player to play in the big leagues since the 1880s. Robinson's impact on the field was immediate, and he was named baseball's Rookie of the Year and would emerge as one of the game's top superstars.

Perhaps the greatest accomplishment of Robinson's career was his role in helping "Dem Bums" to their first and only World Series title, though his contribution was by enabling other African American players rather than his own athletic achievements. That season of 1955 was not a remarkable one for Robinson, who was well into the declining days of his career. Dodgers management tried putting Robinson in a number of positions, but he didn't seem to stick anywhere. He also missed a good chunk of the regular season and, perhaps most bruising, Game Seven of the World Series.

Though Robinson's decline was evident on the field, his inspiration lived on, as in that same season of 1955, Don Newcombe, a teammate of Jackie's, became the first black pitcher to reach the 20-win plateau.

Robinson's spirit continues to be felt today, long after he passed away. His widow, Rachel Robinson, established the Jackie Robinson Foundation, which, as described on Jackie Robinson.com, "offers a $10,000 scholarship toward college tuition for highly motivated minority students."

Recognizing how important Robinson has been both as a figure in baseball and in North American society, Major League Baseball honors his memory every year with Jackie Robinson Day. On that day, every MLB player in every game wears Jackie's number 42. It is the only time the number is ever worn, as the number has been retired by every Major League Baseball team.

While Robinson appeared on some trading cards during his first season that were issued by Bond Bread, he would not earn a classically defined rookie card until 1949. A gum company called Leaf was preparing to enter the baseball card market at the time, and they would make Robinson a part of their collection. There is some confusion in regard to this set as some cards have a 1948 copyright date while others are noted as being from 1949, and most grading companies and hobby price guides call it a 1948–49 issue. The skip-numbered set was a source of frustration for kids at the time, but it has taken on a life of its own in the modern era of collecting, as it is one of the most attractive of the period. Comprised of then-current stars and legends, it is a real challenge to collect, and highly graded copies of the Robinson card are a true treasure.

Also issued in 1949 was Robinson's first Bowman card. After their successful first release the year before, the company moved from primitive black-and-white cards to adding color to the mix, making a real winner for themselves. Collectors will debate until the end of time as to whether or not the Leaf or Bowman card is Robinson's true rookie card, but the actual answer is that both of them deserve the distinction since it has been proven that the Leaf set was not issued in 1948 (and only some of the cards actually bear that copyright date despite their text reflecting the completion of that season).

Which Robinson rookie is more desirable? It depends entirely upon the opinion of the collector, but it seems that the Leaf card is the one to get, due to scarcity and overall attractiveness. As time goes on, the card is unlikely to lose any of its appeal as new generations learn of Robinson's amazing life and he continues to serve as an inspiration to us all. ◀ ◀ ◀

Older cards undergo severe scrutiny as collectors submit their treasures for professional grading.

STEPHEN LAROCHE'S
TOP 10 CARDS

1 ▶ 1954–55 TOPPS GORDIE HOWE

In my opinion, this is the most beautiful trading card of all time, and I acquired mine in 2003 after years of hunting for one at the right price.

2 ▶ 1910–11 C56 LESTER PATRICK

As a teenager, I first began to read about the innovations that Patrick brought to the game of hockey and became obsessed with finding this card. I grabbed one through an online auction in 2006 and probably overpaid for it. . . .

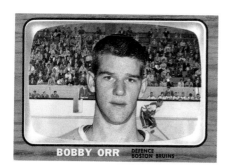

3 ▶ 1966–67 TOPPS BOBBY ORR

To me, this is the most important hockey card of the 1960s, and I was lucky enough to acquire one through a significant trade where I gave up a lot of modern cards to get it. I think I'll come out ahead on the deal in the long run!

4 ▶ 1979–80 O-PEE-CHEE
WAYNE GRETZKY

As a kid, I could never get my hands on this card and I was lucky enough to grab one in terrible condition for $50 in 1991. A little over a decade later, I upgraded it and don't feel the need to do that again.

5 ▶ 1951–52 PARKHURST
"THE WINNING GOAL"

The story of Bill Barilko's tragic end is part of Canada's cultural heritage, and this card captures a legendary moment in history.

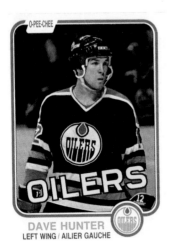

6 ▶ 1981–82 O-PEE-CHEE DAVE HUNTER

My first pack of hockey cards contained one of these, and since I was a huge Edmonton Oilers fan at the time, I was hooked.

7 ▶ 1963–64 PARKHURST GORDIE HOWE

This is a card that I would dream about owning as a child since it just looked amazing. I grabbed mine at a card show in Brockville, Ontario, in 1991 and really should look at upgrading it.

8 ▶ 2004–05 FRANCHISES AUTO KEN WREGGET

Wregget was the first NHL player I ever met as a child, and I was able to sit down with him in 2005 and have him sign these cards for In The Game.

9 ▶ 1991–92 UPPER DECK HULL HOCKEY HEROES AUTOGRAPH

For collectors in 1991–92, this card was almost like an urban myth. You weren't convinced that it existed until you saw one with your own eyes. I didn't spend much to add one to my collection, but it is a definite favorite.

PHIL ROBERTO   left wing

BLUES

10 ▶ 1973-74 O-PEE-CHEE
PHIL ROBERTO

I won't sugarcoat it: I don't think that fighting in hockey is a bad thing. This card that features Roberto laying his fists down on Billy Smith is a must-have for any collector, since it's something you really don't get to see very often on a card. ◀◀◀

JON WALDMAN'S
TOP 10 CARDS

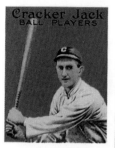

JOE JACKSON, CLEVELAND - AMERICANS

**1 ▶ 1993 CRACKER JACK REPRINTS
"SHOELESS" JOE JACKSON**

My favorite movie and book, so why not my favorite card too? This "Shoeless" card was my must-have and has stayed with me.

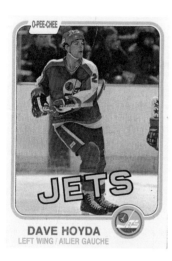

DAVE HOYDA
LEFT WING / AILIER GAUCHE

2 ▶ 1981–82 O-PEE-CHEE DAVE HOYDA

The first card I ever owned. While working at *Canadian Sports Collector*, former Winnipeg Jet Doug Lecuyer emailed me when he saw the card and pointed out that it is him, not Hoyda, who's pictured.

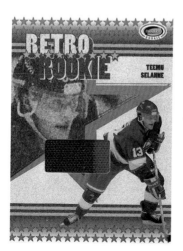

**3 ▶ 2003–04 PARKHURST ROOKIE
TEEMU SELÄNNE JERSEY**

This dual-color jersey card is my favorite among the 800-plus Selanne cards in my collection. Obsessive? You bet.

4 ▶ 2005 LEAF CERTIFIED MATERIALS FABRIC OF THE GAME ROGER MARIS

Living close to Fargo, ND, meant I visited the Maris Hall of Fame annually. Getting his game-used card was a must.

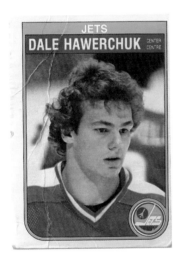

5 ▶ 1982–83 O-PEE-CHEE DALE HAWERCHUK

Though I never got one as a kid, as an adult I now have a couple of my childhood hero. If only I knew back then that Dale was my future wife's neighbor . . .

6 ▶ WWE 2008 ULTIMATE RIVALS SHAWN MICHAELS/ DAVEY BOY SMITH

Working for Topps has been absolutely incredible, partly because I get to pay tribute to guys like Michaels and Smith, two of my favorite wrestlers.

7 ▶ 2005–06 IN THE GAME HEROES AND PROSPECTS MAXIME OUELLET

This was the first time a photo of mine appeared on a card. I'm still trying to get all the variations.

8 ▶ 1909–11 T206 ED REULBACH

I never thought I'd own a T206, but this was a rare find at a reasonable price. Plus, it's a Piedmont back!

9 ▶ 2005 DONRUSS LEATHER AND LUMBER FRANK ROBINSON AUTOGRAPH

I'm a show card nut, so to be able to get a legendary signature from the Hawaii Trade Conference was amazing.

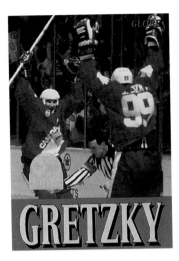

10 ▶ 1995 SEMIC GRETZKY 1987 CANADA CUP

An oddball Swedish release that captures the second most famous goal in Canadian hockey history. ◀◀◀

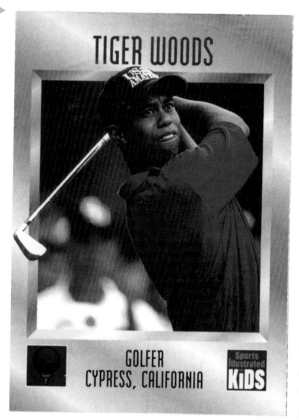

WHEN IS A ROOKIE card not really a rookie card? Well, that is a question many collectors have asked over the years about certain athletes, but there are few cases as confusing as that of Tiger Woods, who has three cards that have been referred to as his first trading card.

The greatest golfer of his, and perhaps any, generation, Woods burst onto the PGA Tour in August 1996, and the folks at *Sports Illustrated for Kids* magazine decided to make a trading card of him for their December 1996 issue. It was a shrewd move on their part, and one that proved quite profitable over time for then-subscribers and speculators. As part of a multi-card sheet bound into the publication, it had to be cut out by hand or separated by perforations. As a result, it is difficult to find in top condition, and professionally graded copies command a significant premium.

The next year, Woods appeared on cardboard once again as a small company called Grand Slam Ventures put out a set featuring players who had won the annual Masters tournament. It was a smash hit at the time since golf cards were becoming a greater curiosity for collectors and there were several parallel

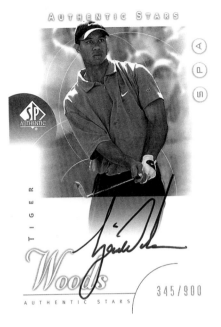

AUTHENTIC STARS

TIGER Woods

345/900

AUTHENTIC STARS

versions. Many thought that this card would be considered his rookie by the market, but it was being distributed as a complete set rather than in pack form, which hurt its qualifications by traditional definitions.

As the legend of Woods began to grow with every tournament victory, it seemed that golf cards were only a step away from becoming a part of the mainstream hobby. In 2001, Upper Deck took the plunge and put together a 200-card set that ensured Woods would be prominently featured — especially in light of an autograph deal they had secured with him. For several months, his cards were the hottest thing around and the editorial staff at Beckett Media made the odd decision to declare his card in the set his rookie issue — much to the confusion and anger of collectors who felt they were simply riding a trend and pandering to one of their largest advertisers.

Despite this, any major card featuring Woods was sure to be a big pull and there was none bigger than his 2001 SP Authentic autographed rookie card. Limited to 900 copies, it was a challenge to get one fresh from a pack and the chance to pull one made the product a hobby favorite. Eight years after it was released, it was selling in the $3,500 range and many consider it to be the most sought-after and popular golf trading card ever.

However, as time went on there appeared to be some issues with the 2001 golf product that are primarily attributed to over-production, and its market value began to soften greatly. It also did not help that Upper Deck and the PGA stopped producing golf cards in 2005.

Nothing like that could compare to what happened in November 2009, when a *National Enquirer* story claimed that

Woods had an extramarital affair. This salacious revelation evolved into a media circus with Woods' mysterious car crash shortly thereafter. As a result, he decided to take a break from golf and his return to the sport did not result in any tournament victories as of 2010.

Today, the 2001 Upper Deck golf "rookie card" can often be found for less than $20 dollars at hobby shops and even less from online sources. As more information about Woods' personal life was publicly revealed and Woods continued to stay away from the game, the value of his trading cards and related memorabilia significantly softened. Upper Deck decided to stand behind one of their marquee spokesmen and, in the long run, it could prove to be either a shrewd move or a tremendous folly but hobbyists who invested in "the world's greatest golfer" are hoping that he will return to the top of his game. ◀◀◀

Cards are still the focal point the hobby, but today's collector will also pick up other memorabilia from their local hobby shop or show.

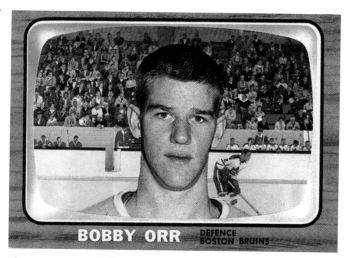

BOBBY ORR
is arguably the greatest defenseman in the history of hockey, for he revolutionized the way his position was played. In the fall of 1966, he joined the Boston Bruins and the fresh-faced recruit with a crew cut made an immediate impact. His early season play ensured that Canadian youth would try to get their hands on his first hockey card when it came out that winter.

At the time, the NHL's Original Six era was coming to an end and the game was beginning to change at a rapid pace. For over a decade the Topps Company had been producing hockey cards for the Canadian market through O-Pee-Chee (based out of London, Ontario). Without any competition from Parkhurst, they could put out a 132-card set that had a neat television design reminiscent of the 1955 Bowman baseball release. (In fact, Topps got some major mileage from the design, as their football set featuring AFL players was released at the time as well.)

What some collectors may not realize is that there are essentially two key versions of the Bobby Orr card with this design. When it was originally issued during the 1966–67 season, Canadian youngsters were able to get the version that was printed by O-Pee-Chee, but American collectors had to wait a little while to get their hands on Orr's freshman card because Topps decided to create a 66-card test version of the set that happened to include the young star.

The exact circumstances of how this test issue was released has often been debated by vintage hockey card enthusiasts, but it was widely speculated that Topps issued the set in time for the 1967–68 NHL season that saw six new U.S.-based clubs hit the ice. The test version of the Orr card features a lighter brown border than the Canadian version and the text on the back is only in English. Produced in much lower quantities, it now commands a serious premium — especially in top condition, since the colored borders are prone to showing the slightest bit of damage.

Orr won the Calder Trophy as the NHL's Rookie of the Year in 1966–67, and as a sophomore the following year he won the Norris Trophy for the first of what would become eight consecutive times as the league's best defenseman. In 1970, he would be responsible for one of the most iconic moments in hockey history as he soared through the air after being tripped up and still managed to score a Stanley Cup–winning goal. Knee woes would hit him at various points in his career, but when he was healthy, he was the sport's dominant player and top box office attraction. As the end of the 1970s approached, he would shockingly sign with the Chicago Blackhawks as a free agent and retire early in the 1978–79 season.

During the formative years of the hockey collectors market, Orr's rookie card was highly sought after and commanded a large premium in the early price guides. Even after his retirement, his legend fueled its soaring market value, and it quickly became one of card collecting's holy grails. There is a major problem with counterfeit versions of the regular card floating around the hobby, so savvy collectors should become familiar with other cards in the set before purchasing or buy one that was slabbed and graded by a respected third-party authenticator. ◀ ◀

COLLECTORS OF TODAY'S SPORTS may not think much of this card making the list. After all, Babe Ruth memorabilia cards, while in relatively short supply, aren't the hardest cards to come by these days. So many baseball series have included game-used equipment from the man simply known as "The Babe" that you're almost more likely to see a set that carries a coveted Ruth piece than one that doesn't.

That wasn't the case, however, near the end of the last millennium. After all, it had only been a scant few years that sports card fanatics had been treated to game-used cards popping out of packs. Predominantly, these cards were of current stars like Ken Griffey Jr. or Kobe Bryant, but the occasional legend was thrown into the mix, such as in hockey where Bobby Hull jerseys were being pulled.

Just a couple short years later though, the Upper Deck Company acquired a Babe Ruth game-used baseball bat and announced that cards would be made with pieces of lumber wielded by one of the greatest players (if not *the* greatest player) ever to lace up cleats for diamond ball. The response from collectors wasn't surprising for a time when questions had begun to arise as to whether or not the companies would quickly slip into the world of going too far in their pursuit of hobby dollars. After all, a Ruth bat was a treasure that, for many fans, was more appropriate to be seen, as a full piece, in Cooperstown or in a museum, not in a baseball card.

Obviously, Upper Deck didn't see the bat the same way. The equipment purchased was a cracked bat and hardly a one-of-a-kind item — many of Ruth's bats had survived over the years in private collections or in the Baseball Hall of Fame. In that respect, especially in comparison with other game-used memorabilia (including one piece that we will talk about further into the book), the Ruth bat card wasn't nearly as controversial as the collecting community was making it out to be.

It's also worth noting that the Ruth bat was not the only piece from a long-ago player that was sliced up for Piece of History. Indeed, the '99 set was a landmark as one of the first, and quite possibly most popular, series that featured players from the 500 home run club. That year also saw Ted Williams, Ernie Banks, Willie Mays and Mickey Mantle bat cards created, as well as a three-bat card of Ruth, Mays and Hank Aaron, then the three all-time leading home run hitters. The 500 home run club set continued over the next few years, adding some legends not previously featured and new inductees into the elite group.

Of course, the bats from Ruth and his compatriots were just the beginning of what would soon become the hottest trend in baseball cards. It didn't take long for more legendary equipment to go under the knife, to the point that now if there is a player whose jersey, pants, bat, glove or other piece of equipment hasn't been included in a card, it either is in the Hall of Fame or is on a shortlist of one of the trading card companies for inclusion somewhere in the near future.

The debate over cutting up legendary memorabilia, it appears, has been won by the card manufacturers, and for collectors who would otherwise never get the opportunity to own a piece of history, such as this card of one of the greatest of all time — Babe Ruth. ◀ ◀

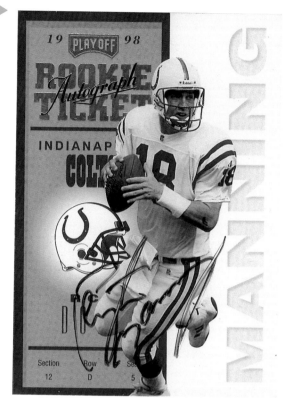

TO TRULY APPRECIATE what Peyton Manning has done in his career thus far, one has to look back to how he started his NFL tenure. You see, the son of Archie Manning was once better known for his parentage than his passing. Sure, he had a fantastic career-opening season, tossing for 3,739 yards and 26 touchdowns, but he also threw a league-leading 28 interceptions.

Still, there was much hope for the number one pick from the 1998 NFL Entry Draft, and certainly more than for the number two pick, Ryan Leaf. Leaf, you may recall, didn't exactly pan out — he played all of four seasons in the NFL and accumulated a QB rating of 50.0 throughout his career, which was marred by a bad attitude and a wrist injury.

Manning, however, would meet and, in the eyes of some, exceed all expectations. As of 2010, Manning had accumulated four MVP awards (more than any player in football history), a Superbowl ring, and a few records (including throwing the most touchdowns in one season before Tom Brady re-broke the mark), arguably making him *the* marquee name in the NFL.

Back in '98, collectors had ample opportunities to pick up Manning rookies. Though the NFL's annual crop of first-year cards was picked up with the same fervor back then as it is now, Manning was seen as someone special that everyone from investors to casual collectors tried to get into their collections.

Unlike with so many superstars before him, the Manning cards provided a multitude of options for even the most discerning palate to choose from. Beckett.com lists an unheard of 502 cards dated for the 1998 season, including an astounding 43 listed rookie cards. Among those RCs, however, you won't find our selection as the premiere card among the mass quantities of first-years from Mr. Manning.

You see, Playoff Inc. was doing something a wee bit ahead of their time in their Rookie Tickets subset — the cards were really, really short-numbered to only 200 copies apiece, plus they were autographed by the depicted rookie.

So at this point, the hobby gods were still appeased. Yes, there was a limited quantity, but it wasn't so severe; a collector, even in that era when online trading was in its infancy, could still acquire it if they searched hard enough.

Instead, the controversy around the card stemmed from how collectors could acquire such a gem — redemption, a.k.a. the single dirtiest word in card-collecting lexicon.

Because the cards weren't immediately able to go from pack to protective holder, hobby brass were reluctant to label it as a rookie card. That didn't matter, however, to most collectors — the card was still one of the hottest on the market, with or without Beckett's RC designation.

1998 was a pivotal year in general for Playoff. That year, Pinnacle Brands, which had previously amassed a card empire by acquiring Donruss/Leaf, filed for Chapter 11 bankruptcy in the United States. Playoff would end up acquiring the brands and become Donruss/Playoff Inc. Years later, the group would also acquire the brands from Pacific Trading Cards Inc., before being taken over by Panini, which had previously been best known for its stickers. ◀◀◀

NEW YORK

JOE NAMATH   quarterback

IT'S A SIMPLE NAME, BUT ONE that perhaps more than any other may be the most honored in all of sports — Joe. This ordinary name has been attached to some of the most extraordinary people in the history of athletic competition. Attach the last name Montana, DiMaggio, Louis or others and an image of sports excellence is sure to pop into one's mind. Perhaps the most famous Joe of all is the one that starred on the gridiron — "Broadway" Joe Namath.

Namath was a player who, amid a decade of change for the United States of America, took football's tradition and turned it 180 degrees. Everything about Namath seemed to go against the grain. His look was more akin to someone you would see on the fields of Woodstock than you would in a football stadium. His swagger and confidence was more showy than most, if not all, traditional players would dare. Even his attire spoke to his rebellious nature — he wore white shoes on the field, as opposed to the traditional black, and donned a fur coat on the sidelines.

And then there's the guarantee. No player would've even dreamed of making a declaration as brash as Namath's prior to Super Bowl III. To have the cojones to declare victory long before you step into battle was simply not done. But that's what was different about Joe Namath — he was fearless. He didn't worry about repercussions.

In that case though, he didn't have to. Perhaps had he failed to lead the Jets into battle and come out on top, Namath would've been chided instead of celebrated, but as the game played out, Broadway Joe pulled off a Kreskin-like feat of foresight.

The victory did more than simply give the Jets their first Vince Lombardi Trophy — it brought a sense of wonderment to the Super Bowl fans, who saw that, indeed, on this given Sunday, anything can happen. One team could appear to be vastly superior, and on paper a blowout could be expected, but as they say, there's a reason why games are played on the field and not on paper.

Namath's rebellious attitude would come to the forefront again soon after Super Bowl III, when he would retire over a dispute over the ownership of his bar, Bachelors III. Rather than sell his stake in the bar, Namath would choose to retire, a big blow to the NFL. But luckily, NFL Commissioner Pete Rozelle and Namath would reach a compromise, allowing Namath to return to the league and complete a legendary career.

It's funny, then, to look at his rookie card and barely see any sign of what lay ahead for the James Dean of the gridiron. In this 1965 card by Topps, Namath, in a posed shot, doesn't yet have the fire in his eyes that would ignite the league — you can only see hope.

Perhaps though, that hope was also in the eyes of the Topps brass, who decided to experiment with card size for the first time in over 10 years. Up until this point, the differences in measurements of cards were minimal, at times less than a half-inch. But for whatever reason, Topps, which was then virtually the only company producing licensed sports cards at all, put out a larger card, roughly one and a half times the size of previous releases. The "Tall Boys" (as they came to be called) would be a one-year experiment that seemed to fall out of favor with collectors.

Interestingly, in the early 1990s, the Tall Boys were reintroduced to the hobby, appropriately first in football by Fleer, who were a constant thorn in Topps's side in baseball. Fleer also held an AFL license from 1960 to 1963, while Topps produced NFL cards. This was before the Philadelphia Gum Co. came on board, taking the NFL license. Topps was then given the AFL license starting in 1964, just one year before Broadway Joe took the stage for the first time.

Ultimately, as Sportsology.net's Director of Communications Russ Cohen explains, Namath's look of hope could be one for a full recovery. "The story that I've heard over the years is pretty cool. Urban legend is he was in the hospital for one of his many surgeries when Topps realized that they needed a picture of him for his card so they put a jersey on him right then and there," Cohen said. ◄ ◄

Can't afford a Namath RC? You can still pick up several of his cards in modern series.

1948 BOWMAN
GEORGE MIKAN

IN 1948, BASKETBALL BECAME THE last of the "big four" sports to have a trading card set when the Bowman Gum Company decided to try something new after releasing football and baseball sets earlier in the year. However, in a bold move, they decided to add some color to the cards and tinted the player portraits.

The set was split into two different series of 36 cards, and the second of the two has proven to be much more difficult to find over time. This second set also contained a key card of young superstar George Mikan of the Basketball Association of America's Minneapolis Lakers. The first true "big man" on the professional scene, most historians of the sport believe that he paved the way for many other superstars who followed. His dominance of opponents was so overwhelming that the NBA would add rules such as widening the foul lane and implementing a shot clock in the interest of fairness.

At 6'11", Mikan, appropriately nicknamed Mr. Basketball, was a force to be reckoned with and he was a part of several championship teams before retiring in 1956. The original #99 would also be named to the NBA's 25th and 35th anniversary teams, be listed as one of the NBA's 50 greatest players in 1996 and earn the impressive moniker of "greatest player of the half century."

After leaving the game, he became the first commissioner of the American Basketball Association and also fought for the rights of retired players and a return of the NBA to Minnesota. As tribute to his efforts in returning the game to the Midwest state, a statue of Mikan was erected outside the Target Center, home to the Minnesota Timberwolves.

As basketball card collecting became a more serious pursuit, the chase for Mikan's only major issue from his playing days became a holy grail quest for hobbyists with deep pockets. High-grade copies of the card are very difficult to find and in November 2009, a copy graded as a PSA 10 went for $186,000 through auction house Memory Lane Inc. To date, it is the only copy of the card to be graded at that level, and a PSA 9 sold for $52,000 the year before.

Bowman's involvement in basketball cards would end as quickly as it began, as Topps bought out the company in the mid-1950s. Topps itself would then have an on-off run of basketball cards over the next several decades until firmly establishing its position in hoops in the 1990s. Once there, Topps resurrected the Bowman brand, using the familiar name to produce sets that, like in other sports, were accentuated by a multitude of rookie cards. The Bowman name would again become extremely popular with collectors during this era, which would last until the 2009–10 season when the NBA and its players association would sign an exclusive agreement with Panini.

Realistically speaking, most collectors will never have an opportunity to own a card that is as big as the original big man himself, but it is without question one of the greatest in the hobby. ◄ ◄

BRONKO
NAGURSKI

FOR SOME SPORTING legends, it almost feels like their ascension to superstardom is a birthright. Look just at the names of some of sport's greatest marquee men and women and you can sense their future dominance.

The best, however, may be that of Bronislau "Bronko" Nagurski. The pride of Rainy River, Ontario, had a name to match that unmistakable aura of toughness he had whenever he stepped onto the field.

Playing offence and defense (as was commonplace in those days) during his college career at the University of Minnesota, Nagurski was played as both a fullback and tackle from 1927 to 1929, and in his last year was named an All-American at both positions.

It was inevitable, then, that Nagurski would get the call to the big leagues, and he soon debuted with a team that would become legendary for its hard-nosed, rough-and-tough style of American football — the Chicago Bears. Playing out of Soldier Field, the Bears and Nagurski seemed like a match made on heaven's gridiron.

With the Bears, Nagurski won two NFL championships. Nagurski primarily played as a running back and on the defensive line, as was the practice in that era. He also served as an offensive lineman, making him the only non-kicker to receive All-Pro honors at three different positions. Nagurski would also spend time in the wrestling ring, becoming a three-time world champion during his football career and later turning to the mat wars full-time after his NFL days were complete.

Nagurski would also be part of the first ever, nationally distributed, dedicated football card set — National Chicle. Made by the gum company of the same name, National Chicle has stood the test of time as the most revered set in all of football history and is home to a plethora of rookie cards from the NFL's all-time greats. Some might say it has more to do with its position as the first ever NFL series, but even without having that title under its belt, the National Chicle series would still be one of the hottest ever created because of the artistic majesty of the cards. The mini paintings are absolutely phenomenal to look at and have stood the test of time, unlike any other set produced for pigskin, or many other sports.

Curiously, despite being an NFL series, many players aren't depicted as part of their professional teams, and this includes Nagurski. It is a Minnesota banner that hangs in the background of his card, representative of his college days. Regardless of this, the Nagurski is treasured by Chicago's faithful as equally as it is by collectors from across the U.S.

So great was Nagurski's impact on the game that today his cards can still be found in packs from most of the major companies. Since the turn of the century, Topps, Panini and Sportkings have all included the legendary player in their products, with many cut autographs being the highlights of these insertions. ◀ ◀

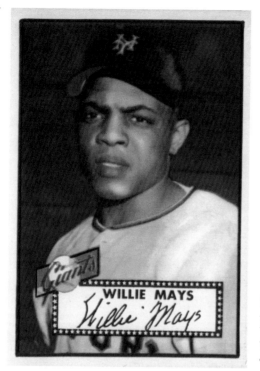

STORIES OF THE "SAY HEY" kid are many, but the one that will forever be told is "The Catch." As famous as any play in sports history, Mays cemented his legacy in sports with an over-the-shoulder nab in the 1954 World Series. A long fly ball off the bat of Vic Wertz was headed to the warning track of the Polo Grounds and seemed like an easy double that would bring in one, if not two, Cleveland Indians for scores in the late stages of game one.

Mays tracked the ball as if he had a radar attached to his arm. He caught the ball in a basket-style grab, shocking fans and opponents alike. The snag prevented what would have most likely led to an Indians victory. Instead, Mays turned out to be a double hero, first with his game-saving catch, then by scoring the game-winning run in the 10th inning. The Giants would go on to win the World Series that year.

That feat alone would have ensured that fans would remember Mays for years to come, but William Howard Mays Jr. was already well on his way to becoming one of the greatest athletes baseball had ever seen. Though the 1951 Rookie of the Year was coming off nearly two seasons away from the professional game due to military service, he made '54 not only his return, but his ascension to the biggest stage of them all. He would play in his first All-Star game and win his first of two National League MVP awards.

But back when this card was issued in 1952, his 1954 triumphant return seemed like an eternity away for Giants fans (at this point, the team was still in New York). Part of the infamous Topps series that was partly destroyed, the Mays card would inevitably be in high demand, coming off his Rookie of the Year honors, but Topps didn't release it right away, perhaps to build momentum for the later issues. The card, along with Mickey Mantle's piece, was a phenom in the industry, lying in wait for eager kids to pull.

Also in similarity to the Mantle, Mays's Topps card was not his rookie, as Bowman beat Topps to the punch in 1951 and issued the card just as Mays was making his debut. But it is the '52 Topps card that is the classic for collectors.

Following the '54 comeback season, Mays proved that his return was not a fluke. In total, Mays racked up 24 All-Star game selections, 12 consecutive Gold Glove awards, another National League MVP award and would be named to Major League Baseball's All-Century team.

Despite all the accolades, Mays's career is still defined largely by "The Catch" — one single play out of the hundreds that he made in all his years in the majors. Over the years, a number of collectibles have commemorated that play, including a 2002 Topps Tribute game-used memorabilia card, which contains a swatch of Mays's fielding glove and Wertz's bat. The card also features a photo of the Mays catch.

Despite this unique piece and others, for one reason or another, it is the '52 Topps card, that collectors cling to like a child to a security blanket, and the piece today ranks among the greatest baseball cards ever produced. ◀ ◀

ORIOLES
3rd BASE **CAL RIPKEN**

IF A COLLECTOR WAS ASKED in 1990 if they knew what the most valuable regular issue baseball card of the 1980s was, odds are that they would have said something along the lines of the rookie cards of Don Mattingly, José Canseco or even Ken Griffey Jr., but time has proven that the 1982 Topps Traded issue of Cal Ripken Jr. is the decade's essential baseball pasteboard.

Relatively undervalued until the peak of the boom years, Topps's first card of Ripken by himself came in their second annual Traded set, a boxed collection that was available through hobby outlets. He did appear on a multi-player rookie card in their flagship series earlier in the year but his strong play as a freshman ensured that he would get one all to himself a few months later. It should also be noted that the values of his Fleer and Donruss issues from that year pale by comparison, since it is has always been assumed that the Topps Traded set was produced in much smaller quantities.

Former card company executive and editor of *Canadian Sports Collector* Baron Bedesky offered his thoughts on the phenomenon surrounding the Ripken rookie card and the significance of the arrival of Traded sets in the hobby. "The Traded sets, when they were first issued by Topps, were almost considered as afterthoughts by most collectors, something primarily of interest to completists but in many purists' eyes, not a legitimate part of the set because they weren't available in wax packs," he said. "So not a lot was thought of the 1982 version when it initially came out. It took a couple of years for the set to pick up momentum and for the rookie cards in these boxed sets to gather more attention. Of course, Ripken's emergence as a star — he was a key part of the Orioles 1983 World Championship club — combined with the groundswell of popularity building for card collecting in the mid- to late-1980s served as sort of a perfect storm for these boxed sets. Suddenly they were in demand, and just as suddenly the price began to jump by leaps and bounds. The fact that there were three companies producing cards at the time, breaking the longstanding Topps monopoly, also added fuel to the fire. It took a while, but it was a case of right time, right place."

The "Iron Man" proved to be one of the game's most consistent performers and by the end of the '80s, he was considered one of baseball's best. As Ripken began to close in on Lou Gehrig's consecutive games record, the card started to really take off, and it was white hot when he broke the record in 1995. Considering that this feat was only slightly removed from the strike that prematurely ended the 1994 campaign, his class and skill transcended all of the bad feelings harbored by fans, and his quest for immortality made many of them return to the game they once loved.

Once Ripken retired in 2001, it was only a matter of time before he would be enshrined in the Baseball Hall of Fame. His love for the game harkened back to a simpler time and fans still actively pursue his collectibles a decade later. While we can't go back in a time machine to get these cards at rock-bottom prices, the Topps Traded rookie card has settled at a reasonable price in the $120 range. Can we say that about the other big names from that era? Not a chance, and it's likely that this card will remain the decade's best baseball card for many years to come. ◀ ◀

1989 FLEER
BILL RIPKEN

QUITE OFTEN, THERE IS a fine line between fame and infamy. Baseball player Bill Ripken was certainly famous in 1988 as a player for the Baltimore Orioles — not to mention the fact that his brother and teammate, Cal, was one of the sport's biggest stars and a future Hall of Fame member. The brothers were managed by their father, Cal Sr., and the trio was lauded despite the fact that the club was mired at the bottom of the standings in the American League's East Division.

The younger Ripken's transcendence into infamy is memorable even for people who did not collect trading cards; he became the center of attention in the hobby due to two little words written on the knob of his bat and caught on film when a photographer from Fleer came to take the photos for their 1989 set. Since many people consider the words "Fuck Face" to be obscene, the fact that they appeared on something as wholesome and innocuous as a baseball card put the hobby at the center of a media maelstrom, and collectors and dealers alike attempted to capitalize on the controversy. There was even an episode of *The People's Court* on May 24, 1989, that saw the parents of two children fight over the card after the defendant had acquired it from the plaintiff for a dollar when it had a supposed market value of $50. (For the record, Judge Wapner made sure that the Ripken card was returned to the plaintiff's collection.) At one point, the unaltered card was trading as high as $300 on the secondary market.

Fleer quickly stopped the presses in order to save face. The company made several attempts to properly cover up the obscenity and as a result, several variations have been uncovered over the years. These range from the common black box to the white and black scribbled-out versions to the whiteout version that looks as if there was correction fluid placed on that portion of the card.

Boston-based photographer Steve Babineau was working for Fleer at the time and was the shooter on the day where Ripken made history. "On that particular day, he was the only Orioles player to come out for batting practice in his full uniform," he said. "Due to me being taller [6'4"] than him, I had to kneel down a little to get a good shot of him that day."

At this time, Fleer's proofing process had changed from sending out contact sheets to using a blueprint method. It was only after the Fleer cards went to press that Babineau found out about a problem with the photo. He received a call from a company executive who asked if he had heard about an issue with the card. "After looking at the sheet with a loupe, my first internal reaction was that this was bad," he recalled. "My second reaction was that this was going to sell a lot of cards. He asked me to go look at *USA Today*, so I saw the story and told him that he was going to sell a ton of cards!"

Despite initially claiming that he had been the victim of a prank, Ripken later admitted publicly that he had written the offending obscenity on the bat. Shortly after the story hit, he did apologize to Babineau. The photographer recalled, "He came up to me, put an arm around me and said, 'Thanks for making my cards go from five cents to 30 bucks!'"

Fleer was no stranger to correcting errors, as there were several cards in their 1981 and 1982 sets that were changed after the initial print run was released. Some of the originals are still highly sought-after, especially the 1982 John Littlefield card that features a reversed negative.

Needless to say, the Ripken card has acquired a cult following over the years. It is celebrated online at BillRipken .com, a site operated by collector Donovan Ryan that catalogs every known variant and provides collectors with original articles about the hype.

No one seems to know how many of the "Fuck Face" cards were released into the marketplace, but suffice it to say, there are still probably enough of them out there to satisfy the curiosity of those who want one. In fact, they can be found for far less than they were trading for 20 years ago. ◀ ◀

Companies proof cards thoroughly to ensure that no more "Fuck Face" incidents occur.

MANY CONSIDER HIM TO BE among the greatest players of all time, and few would argue that in his generation, no one had a finer swing. But to know Ted Williams' hobby love is to know that the Splendid Splinter was not only a spectacular athlete and a very fan-friendly player, but he was also more richly attached to the collecting world than perhaps any other athlete in history.

You see, Williams wasn't just a player who'd appear at trade shows to sign cards — at one point he owned his own company.

Back in 1993, a group of rogue ex-employees of the Upper Deck Company, along with Williams and his son, John Henry, created a new card business that paid tribute to the legends of the sport. The sets were fairly popular, but the company didn't stick around long in the industry. Today, many of the Ted Williams Co. cards can be found for pennies in most card stores.

Had the company continued, you'd imagine that they would have paid tribute to Williams' rookie card, which was issued in the first of three Play Ball series by Goudey. The series ceased when the United States entered World War II, as did the baseball careers of Williams and other major leaguers, who stopped playing the game to fight for their country.

Goudey took a brave step forward with its Play Ball series. At the time, most sets were art reproductions. Instead, Play Ball featured photography. As one of the first mass-market trading card series, it was undoubtedly a risk; after all, the company had gone the art way a few years earlier and the result was beautiful, colorful renderings that were more eye-catching than an uncolored photograph.

Despite this, the Play Ball series delivered. Many stars had their first cards in the Play Ball sets, but none reached out to the set builder like Williams, who, despite the fact that it was his first year in the league, was already wowing crowds.

As odd as it was for the era, Williams had a card the same year he debuted. It may not seem like a big deal today, where sometimes an RC will be issued years before a player appears in their first professional game, but back then it was a true rarity.

Of course, Williams would go on to have a Hall of Fame–level career and, with all respect to Dan Marino, was the greatest player to never win a league championship. The Curse of the Bambino hung above Ted's time in baseball and is the only blemish on an otherwise stellar career. He would retire as a member of the 500 home run club and a two-time Triple Crown winner and become a Cooperstown inductee.

Since his retirement, he's appeared in several series, including his own Ted Williams Co. card and Upper Deck's Baseball Heroes, which honored him as one of its first releases. He was also the source of controversy around the same time, as Topps, who had reproduced their landmark 1954 series as a reprint edition, could not include Williams because he was exclusive to UD. As a result, Upper Deck produced the card needed to complete this set.

Through all of the controversy, Williams has remained a hot commodity in the hobby, especially this card, his first ever. ◀ ◀

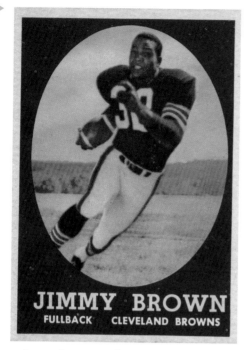

IT CAN BE ARGUED THAT Jim Brown had a greater impact on the game of professional football than any other player in history, and for many football card collectors, his rookie card is considered a must-have item.

A multi-sport athlete who starred at Syracuse University, Brown was taken with the first overall pick in the 1957 NFL draft by the Cleveland Browns and he made an immediate impression with fans and foes alike by leading the league in rushing yards as a rookie. Realistically though, Brown could have been rookie of the year in any sport he pursued. In his high school days, he lettered 13 times, being a standout in track, baseball, lacrosse (for which he was named to the sport's hall of fame) and, of course, football.

For Topps's 1958 football set, it was a no-brainer to include Brown in the collection. His rookie shows him in full flight but without a helmet, since the company often relied on posed shots at the time instead of game action. It is by far the standout in the 132-card set, but is particularly undervalued in comparison to top rookie cards in other sports from the same era.

Over the next few seasons, Brown proved to be difficult to tackle and almost impossible to stop, setting records for most rushing yards in a season and in a career. While both standards were broken in subsequent years, there is no denying that he revolutionized the game. While he only starred for nine seasons, he would lead the league in rushing eight times, setting the record for running yards and rushing TDs in the process, and leading the Browns to their last NFL title in 1964. Brown also was a three-time NFL MVP, had eight All-Pro First Team selections and one Second Team nod. His retirement came as a huge surprise to all, as it seemed as if he could have continued playing for many years.

Elected to the Pro Football Hall of Fame in 1971, the College Football Hall of Fame in 1995 and named to the NFL's 75th Anniversary All-Time Team, Brown's post-football career kept him in the public eye with a number of television and film appearances. He even toyed with the idea of coming out of retirement in 1983 but ultimately stayed off the gridiron.

Collectors recently had the opportunity to obtain cello packs of the 1958 release when a bunch of the rare unopened gems were uncovered during a taping of *Antiques Roadshow* in 2005. The fact that they survived intact so long is mind-boggling, and two years later one pack from this find with the Brown card on the front was sold by Heritage Auctions for $3,107 before any buyer's premium was added.

In 2002, the *Sporting News* declared Brown to be the greatest professional football player ever and as time goes on, there is little doubt that his rookie card is not just a solid investment, but a genuine piece of history that is quite a bargain at any price. ◄ ◄

1936 WORLD WIDE GUM
JOE DIMAGGIO

No. 51 JOE DI MAGGIO

FOR MOST COLLECTORS, Joe DiMaggio's legacy speaks for itself and adding any of his vintage cards to one's collection is a savvy move, as they are a sound investment. However, there has been a fair bit of debate over the years as to which of his early baseball cards is his rookie issue.

Some collectors firmly believe that the 1936 World Wide Gum DiMaggio card is his true rookie card, but there is also some evidence that suggests that the card may not be what it seems. Issued by the Canadian gum company of the same name, the set is often believed to have been released in 1936, but doubt arises as collectors look at the backs of some of the later cards in the series, featuring minor league players, and see where those players were plying their trade at the time. All of a sudden, it seems that the set may in fact have been issued in 1937 instead, which is the season that other DiMaggio cards started to hit the market.

The theory of the World Wide Gum set being issued in 1937 gained some momentum in 2003 as it was proven that what was once considered the 1936–37 World Wide Gum hockey set was actually produced during the 1937–38 season. Only further research will reveal the exact date of issue, but the hobby will hopefully react accordingly in the face of any new evidence.

The fact also remains that despite its incredible scarcity,

the World Wide Gum set is incredibly unattractive to most collectors. The set pales in comparison to other designs from the era and many collectors may prefer to chase his Play Ball cards instead or even the 1938 Goudey Heads Up card since they are more readily available.

Once DiMaggio made his debut with the Yankees in 1936, the club would reel off four consecutive World Series victories, and he became one of the most beloved players in baseball history. In 1941, he hit safely in 56 consecutive games, establishing a standard that may never be broken. After serving in World War II, he returned to baseball and still performed at a high level until his retirement in 1951. He would remain in the public eye for the rest of his life and is also remembered for his marriage to starlet Marilyn Monroe and for acting as a pitchman for Mr. Coffee. His memorabilia and signatures were highly coveted by collectors throughout the world, and he was one of the first players to appear at trading card shows to sign autographs.

No matter which vintage card of DiMaggio that a collector acquires, it will always be money well spent. Naturally, those that are professionally graded and in the best condition will remain the most popular and command the most dollars but the overall scarcity of pre-war baseball cards ensure that his cards in any condition at all will be strong sellers. The hobby will also continue to debate over his true rookie card, and it's likely that a consensus will never be reached. ◀ ◀

THE MONTREAL CANADIENS ARE HOCKEY'S most historic franchise, having originally been welcomed into the old National Hockey Association in 1909. After a dismal first season, they went to great lengths to acquire a new goaltender and found a young prospect named Georges Vézina, who was playing in Chicoutimi, Quebec, at the time.

The club would not need another goalie for many years after the quiet young star made his professional debut on December 31, 1910, against the Ottawa Senators. He was one of the best players in the league that year, as he had the lowest goals-against average among netminders and also helped the Canadiens become a .500 team with a record of 8–8.

During Vézina's second season with Montreal, Imperial Tobacco put out its second series of small hockey trading cards that were inserted into packs of cigarettes. Often referred to by its *American Card Catalog* call number of C55, the set features an ornate design and is made up of 45 cards from NHA clubs. The Vézina rookie card is considered the greatest of them all and shows the young goalie in a posed portrait that was also used on a postcard issued by the company around the same time. The postcards are even more scarce than the C55 cards and a complete set sold for $140,607 when offered up by Classic Auctions in February 2009.

Vézina would go on to great success in Montreal and back-stopped the team to their first Stanley Cup championship during the 1915–16 season. Two more titles would come after the team became a charter member of the National Hockey League in 1917 and the goalie did not miss a single game until early in the 1925–26 season. During Montreal's first game that year, on

November 28, 1925, Vézina collapsed on the ice and was forced to walk away from the sport he loved. A little over four months later, he died from tuberculosis, and the team donated a trophy in his honor that is used to annually recognize the NHL's top goaltender to this day.

There is a great deal of mystery surrounding the life of Vézina and many urban legends would surface over the years. Canadiens owner Leo Dandurand once remarked to the press that his goalie fathered 22 children and did not speak a word of English, but the reality was that he had two children and spoke a minimal amount of the language in order to communicate with teammates. When he was away from the rink, he operated a tannery in his hometown of Chicoutimi and by all accounts lived a very quiet life.

Collectors have very few options when it comes to vintage cards of Vézina but there are a number of modern issues that pay tribute to his contributions to the game of hockey, primarily by In The Game. It is also interesting to note that a Vézina autograph has not been publicly offered for sale, although they do exist. ◀◀

1981 TOPPS
JOE MONTANA

HEADING INTO THE HOBBY'S boom years, there was no bigger player in the minds of football collectors than Joe Montana. A four-time Super Bowl champion at the dawn of the 1990s, he was heavily collected and people already viewed him as a future Hall of Famer, even with his career only just over a decade old.

Of all the Montana cards on the market at that time, none was as popular as his rookie card from the 1981 Topps set. The company had missed out on including him in their set the previous year, but that was understandable since in this era it was common to see a player's first trading card appearance during their second season in the league. Despite the fact that he only started seven games during the 1980 season, Montana led the NFL in pass completion percentage — a mere glimpse of what he would end up accomplishing in 1981. He was named the Most Valuable Player of Super Bowl XVI as the San Francisco 49ers defeated the Cincinnati Bengals by a score of 26–21.

At the time this rookie card was released, Topps was only licensed to show players on football cards and logos are noticeably absent. This was the last season for incompletely licensed NFL cards, but in the current era of collecting, partially licensed cards are becoming popular once again and it is strange to see such trends repeating themselves.

Tracy Hackler, former publisher for Beckett Media, has high

praise for the card and summed up its significance in the hobby world. "Joe Montana's rookie card is one of the three or four most influential football cards of all time," he said. "Thanks immeasurably to the big-game exploits of the man on it, this card was football's most sought after investment target for most of the 1980s, the golden era of modern sports cards. To many, Montana is arguably the greatest quarterback in professional football history; it's only fitting that [the value of] his rookie card signifies that."

Montana was a collegiate star at Notre Dame and was a third round pick in the 1979 NFL draft. During the four Super Bowl victories that he was a part of, he would be named the game's Most Valuable Player three times. An effective quarterback throughout his career, he ranked ninth in all-time passing touchdowns at the end of the 2009 season. An eight-time Pro Bowler, he spent most of his career in San Francisco before joining the Kansas City Chiefs for two seasons. He retired after the 1994 season and was inducted into the Pro Football Hall of Fame in 2000.

In 2009, the first copy of this card that was graded at the pristine 10 level by Beckett Grading Services was offered up for sale by Modern Marvels Auctions and sold for an incredible $65,880. While it is extremely likely that investors may never see additional copies in that condition sell for that price, it was an indication that hobbyists were once again looking at classic trading cards from the 1980s as investment pieces.

Overall, this card is a fairly safe pickup for collectors as Montana's gridiron legacy remains intact more than 15 years after he played his final NFL game. Ungraded copies are relatively affordable, and while there is less competition for the card now compared to in his playing days, there is still some demand for it and that trend should continue over the next few years. ◀ ◀

TOP 11 HOBBY INNOVATIONS

THERE HAVE BEEN A NUMBER of notable innovations to the card collecting world since 1990, but we felt there were some that deserved to be recognized above others.

1 ▶ THIRD-PARTY GRADING

For the investors who remained in the hobby after the boom years, there needed to be something valuable to chase after that would command huge dollars, and that came with the gradual acceptance of third-party grading. Cards that received the highest grades commanded some serious dollars, and while some collectors were apprehensive of the trend, it has been accepted by most.

2 ▶ THE ONLINE WORLD

The boom years were over by 1996, but once people throughout the world discovered the usefulness of the Internet for growing or selling their collections, the survival of the trading card industry was ensured. Whether it is through message boards, card company websites or even auction sites like eBay, collectors are more connected to the industry today. Many collectors have even started hobby-related blogs and information has become instantly available and accessible to all those with an Internet connection. Most card companies are very responsive, using message boards, Facebook and Twitter to connect with collectors, and direct consumer input has allowed card companies to create even greater products.

However, the expansion of the hobby into the online realm has reduced the number of brick and mortar card shops, since online sales are more profitable for dealers. There has also been an increased sense of collector entitlement where people are more vocal about what they demand from card companies. Also, the woes of print media have extended to the hobby; some publications have ceased to exist or cut back on what they produce. They often can't compete with the immediacy of online information and will need to continue to adapt as technology changes.

3 ▶ LIMITED INSERTS

One of the most enduring trends from the latter portion of the boom years is limited insert cards. They can be found in most sets to this day and are generally regarded as cards that are not a part of the base set. While the concept of the "chase card" was once king in the hobby, it has been surpassed in popularity by autographs and game-used memorabilia cards.

4 ▶ PREDICTORS

In the mid-1990s, Upper Deck had an interesting idea: offering up insert cards that could be sent in for a special set if the depicted player accomplished a certain feat. It was revolutionary at the time since collectors had the difficult choice of sending a card in for something or hanging on to the card in the hopes that it would appreciate more value in the long run since so many others were redeemed. The company would utilize the concept once in a while over the next few years, but it seems to have run its course even with the option of making a card redeemable online.

5 ▶ SERIAL NUMBERING

It's one thing for a card company to publicly state what a card is limited to and another thing entirely to let a collector know exactly which card they have in a print run. When manufacturers started to do this, they also created an additional market for cards with a serial number denoting the first or last card in a run along with that which matches the player's uniform number. While some products have gone overboard with serial numbering, like the old SPx Finite brand, it is an aspect of the hobby that is here to stay.

6 ▶ PRESS PLATES

For many collectors, the idea of owning a piece of the printing plate used to create a trading card is an appealing new hobby offshoot. In the late 1990s, Pinnacle started to offer up these one-of-one treasures and they commanded huge dollars at the time. After a lull, they started to become mainstream again in 2002, but their proliferation has resulted in softened prices.

7 ▶ CERTIFIED AUTOGRAPHS

We touched on a couple of certified autograph cards in the big list, but this innovation has really driven the hobby in recent years. Companies were slow to embrace the trend during the boom, but by 1994, they were ready to create one-auto-per-pack releases that, while expensive, cut right to the chase (pardon the pun). Now, it is incredibly rare to see a product come out without some sort of autograph program, but collectors never seem to tire of the trend.

8 ▶ GAME-USED MEMORABILIA

The post-boom years saw card companies scramble to try to find the next big idea, and that came in the form of incorporating pieces of game-used memorabilia into cards. At first these cards weren't easy to pull and commanded huge dollars, but as more collectors demanded better odds of pulling these cards, it got to the point where some products would offer one gamer per pack. As a result, the market was flooded and you can sometimes get one of these cards for as little as a penny plus shipping on eBay. Some current players and vintage stars can still generate hefty premiums, but the game-used memorabilia card is now a hobby fixture and a part of most releases.

9 ▶ DECOYS

With the rise of game-used memorabilia cards, it became apparent that some unsavory types could feel packs and locate one of the prized pieces inside without even needing to open it up. As a result, manufacturers listened to the demands of collectors and began inserting pieces of cardboard with the same thickness of the game-used cards. Some companies even create redemption programs around them to give people something extra for their loyalty. The results of the initiative have been overwhelmingly positive, although pack searching is still one of the hobby's dirty little secrets.

10 ▶ CUT AUTOGRAPHS

The idea of opening up a pack and getting a card with the signature of a long-deceased sports legend is one of the best innovations of the past decade or so and card companies have all been supportive of the cut signature concept. By embedding an authentic signature into a card, they create something special.

In 2001, the collecting world began to buzz over the idea that a manufacturer would charge $100 or more for a single pack of cards. It was scandalous and unheard of at the time, but the trend has since risen to even crazier heights. While the products are often quite limited at this price point or higher, collectors always seem to want something that has the illusion of value and the potential for the pull of a lifetime. The $100 threshold has now soared over $500, but the reality is that we are still buying pretty cardboard pictures . . . even if there are pieces of material and writing on them! ◀ ◀

26 TO 50

A DECADE AFTER BOWMAN'S release of the first major basketball trading card set, Topps decided to revisit the idea, and it proved to be a landmark issue. It featured some of the game's top talent, but at the time, there may not have been any better than a young star for the Boston Celtics named Bill Russell.

In his second pro season, Russell was named the league's Most Valuable Player and the Celtics were on the cusp of becoming the most dominant team of the 1960s. While wearing the iconic green and white jersey, he would be a part of 11 championship teams and eventually become a member of the Hall of Fame. Russell knew how to win, and his defensive skills were among the best ever to be seen on the hardcourt.

The 1957–58 Topps set was a notable achievement for the time — many cards featured game-action photography, and looking at them today, they open a window onto an era when basketball was less glitzy and driven by marketing. At 80 cards, the set featured rookie offerings for numerous other future Hall of Famers, but Russell's is regarded as the cream of the crop.

Considered a challenging set to complete, it also suffered from centering issues and ink problems on the front that resulted in a snowy look on many cards. The main problem, however, may have been sales; Topps stepped away from producing another mainstream basketball set until the 1969–70 campaign. Collectors would not see another major issue released until 1961–62, when Fleer issued a set for only one season. Recognizing Russell's hobby impact, the Philadelphia-based card marker would issue two cards of the Celtic superstar in that product.

Part of the enduring appeal of the Russell card stems from the fact that his relationship with the sports memorabilia industry was frosty during the boom years, but he slowly warmed up to the idea of being involved in a variety of projects. For many years, you simply had to rely on vintage sets to find a card of the retired superstar and that drove up the value of those depicting him. At this point, there are options that include autographs and pieces of game-used memorabilia, but the card to have will always be his rookie issue.

Dr. Brian Price, president of Sportkings LP, worked hard to ensure that Russell was going to be a part of their Sport Kings Series A release and offered his thoughts on Russell's significance in the hobby: "Russell was one of the most dominant players in NBA history and collectors have not had a lot of options over the years to pick up his cards or autographs due to his apprehension toward the sports memorabilia industry. He was a natural choice to be added to our first Sportkings release in 2007, and when I ran into him in the Directors Lounge at the Air Canada Centre during a Toronto Raptors game later on, he thanked me for making him a part of my set. It was a thrill to get a chance to speak with him. He's a wonderful ambassador for his sport." ◄◄◄

1963 ROOKIE STARS

PEDRO GONZALEZ
N. Y. YANKEES, 2B

KEN McMULLEN
L. A. DODGERS, 3B

PETE ROSE
CINCINNATI REDS, 2B

AL WEIS
CHI. WHITE SOX, SS

FOR A TIME, THERE WERE FEW cards bigger in this hobby than the rookie card of Pete Rose, but his fall from grace and subsequent behavior has tarnished his legacy in the eyes of some, and as a result, the once-solid investment doesn't have the power it once had or even potentially could have had.

Kids growing up between the 1960s and 1980s had a genuine idol in Rose when he starred for the Cincinnati Reds, Philadelphia Phillies and Montreal Expos, and as the hobby began to grow, there was a lot of interest in his cards. Naturally, the hottest of Rose's cards was his rookie year release from 1963. This card came in an era when Topps would routinely feature multiple fresh faces on a single card, and the Rose was no exception; he shared space with three other players — Al Weis, Ken McMullen and Pedro González.

But no matter what piece of cardboard bore Rose's likeness, they were all white-hot in the mid-1980s. The rookie card is also notable for being one of the first to be counterfeited, starting a disturbing trend that still continues to this day, where some "collectors" will recreate famous cards and then sell or trade them, passing them off as the real thing.

Rose came up with the Reds in 1963 and would help the team to consecutive World Series victories in 1975 and 1976. After a stint with Philadelphia that saw him win another championship, he spent part of the 1984 season with the Expos before returning to his hometown of Cincinnati where he would serve as the club's manager in addition to stepping out onto the field. In 1985, he was chasing down baseball's all-time hits record and smashed Ty Cobb's standard on September 11 of that year. He retired from active play the following season and acted exclusively as the team's manager.

By 1989, there were grumblings that "Charlie Hustle" had been involved in betting on games, and after an investigation by Major League Baseball, he was banned for life by the sport's power brokers. Public reaction ranged from smug satisfaction to unbridled outrage, but Rose would make a career out of raising the ire of folks like Bud Selig. While he initially claimed some level of innocence, he would eventually admit that he placed bets on games. As a result, the Baseball Hall of Fame declared him ineligible for induction, but he was still voted to the MLB All-Century Team in 1999.

Since no licensed trading card manufacturer had actively produced trading cards of Rose since 1989 (outside of a single card issued by Upper Deck), there was a void in the hobby. As a result, the value of many of his cards began to soften, but there was a glimmer of hope in 2007 as the relaunched Sportkings boldly signed Rose to a deal, creating a hobby sensation. The high-end multi-sport product would include certified autographs and pieces of game-used memorabilia.

"A tribute to Pete Rose was long overdue," said Sportkings LP President Dr. Brian Price. "It's only fitting that a player of his stature would appear in our premier release. MLB would not allow their licensees to use him for trading cards, so we did him. At Sportkings, we care about what a player does inside the lines, not outside of them."

Other companies would follow the lead of Sportkings: Panini signed Rose the following year and Upper Deck worked out a deal with him after they lost their Major League Baseball license in 2009.

As far as investments go, the Rose rookie card is one that seems to be solid and has some potential for growth if there is a change of heart by Major League Baseball and they allow him to return to the game he loves so much. High grade copies go at a healthy premium due to the condition sensitivity of the card, and there is a lot of nostalgia for the fallen hero's glory days that helps buoy its secondary market value. ◄ ◄ ◄

*Rose's rookie has an unmistakable visual appeal, as do many
other vintage baseball cards.*

Gordie Howe Right Wing

DETROIT RED WINGS

BY THE TIME TOPPS DECIDED to enter the hockey card market, they had already established themselves as the producers of quality baseball, football and non-sports cards — not to mention the unforgettable gum that was included in each pack. However, there was one little problem in the fact that the American market wasn't quite ready to accept hockey cards.

With all the uncertainly stateside, Topps chose to distribute their first hockey effort through O-Pee-Chee in Canada. The set is considered to be one of the most beautiful of any era. The set was made up of 60 players from the four American NHL clubs — the Boston Bruins, Chicago Blackhawks, Detroit Red Wings and New York Rangers; you weren't getting players from the Montreal Canadiens and the Toronto Maple Leafs — but the end result was pure magic. Available in one-cent and five-cent packs, they were in direct competition with the Parkhurst set that contained all of the Original Six clubs, but time has ultimately proven that collectors prefer the Topps set due to its overall beauty.

By this card's 1954–55 release, Gordie Howe had established himself as one of hockey's elite superstars by helping the Red Wings to three Stanley Cup titles (and he would earn another at the close of the season). In addition, he led the NHL in scoring for the fourth time in his career in 1953–54 and had won the Hart Trophy as the league's Most Valuable Player twice. Needless to say, the Canadian kids (and some American kids, too!) were quite happy to pull his card out of this exciting new product.

Over time, the 1954–55 Topps Gordie Howe has gained a cult following and there are a large number of collectors who firmly believe that this hockey card is the most beautiful ever produced. The blue bottom borders often make it difficult to locate high-grade copies, though dealers rarely have trouble moving them at any price or in any condition. Fortunately for collectors on a budget, there are some affordable alternatives in the form of authorized reprints issued by Topps during the 1998–99 season.

The company would also revisit the design of this card for its 2000–2001 debut Heritage release. A critical and commercial success, that release also brought back the bubblegum to hockey collectors who had gone a decade without finding a sickeningly sweet pink slab in their packs.

To further pay homage to the original series, the Heritage sets also included reproductions of select original cards with autographs or swatches from stadium seats. Among these were Gordie Howe cards, which included pieces from a chair at the Olympia Arena in Detroit, as well as a signature card that books far higher than any other in the set.

As a hockey card investment, the 1954–55 Topps Gordie Howe has seen slow but steady growth and is about as sound as they come. As time goes on and new generations of collectors learn about Howe's on-ice accomplishments, they are sure to have some interest in his card, and many hobbyists believe it is one of the top five post-war, pre-boom cards issued. ◄ ◄

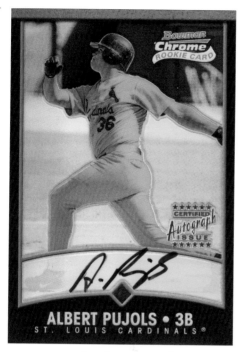

IT'S HARD TO IMAGINE THAT any card in the midst of baseball's darkest days — the steroid era — would appear on this list; yet a few were able to crack our lineup, most notably this issue by Topps.

Before we get into the card itself, it's worth reviewing Bowman's rejuvenated hobby status. Back in the 1950s, Topps and Bowman were separate companies that, while not living harmoniously, were both key producers in the baseball card market. To say that competition between the two was big would be as much an understatement as saying the New York Yankees and Boston Red Sox have a mild distaste for one another.

Eventually, Topps was able to gain supremacy and did what every company dreams of doing — it bought its competition. For decades, the Bowman name, which had long been synonymous with baseball, was dormant. It wasn't until 1989, in fact, that Topps decided to bring it out of retirement, just in time for the hobby's boom period. The brand was used first in baseball, just in time for Ken Griffey Jr.'s rookie card campaign, and later in hockey, football and basketball.

The magic, however, wasn't there. For whatever reason, Bowman didn't strike initially with collectors. It wasn't until 1992, in fact, that the name started to pick up steam. That year, Topps announced that it was drastically cutting production of the set, which was fine with collectors . . . that is, until they saw that rookie cards of future MLB stars like Mike Piazza were popping out of packs from that set — and that set only.

Yes, Topps had successfully used their grandfathered contract of signing players individually, rather than the group licensing of the MLB Players Association, allowing them to get rookies in their sets way before Upper Deck, Donruss/Playoff/ Pinnacle, Fleer or any other company, and, as the tagline goes, Bowman indeed became the "Home of the Rookie Card."

Topps wasn't done with just issuing the Bowman cards, however. After seeing success in the Topps Chrome product (essentially a heavily UV-coated version of the regular series with some embossing effects), the technology was brought over to the Bowman line. To make cards that much more desirable, elite prospects were part of a special autographed subset.

The recipe for success worked wonders, especially for the Pujols card. In 2001, Pujols was a young buck with the St. Louis Cardinals and seemed destined for greatness. That prediction indeed came true, as Pujols, arguably MLB's player of the decade for the 2000s, won three National League MVP awards, a World Series ring and numerous other accolades.

When you combine the production value of the card and Pujols' success, you get one of the most in-demand rookie cards produced in baseball in the last decade. This card, made even more valuable by its limited run of just 500 copies, has continually sold well into the four figures.

With a card gaining so much attention and commanding such high dollar values, it would seem inevitable that an unsavory character would take the opportunity to produce fake versions, as was way too common practice during the boom era of the hobby. And yes, even with technologically advanced production methods, reports surfaced in September 2009 that fake cards were indeed being circulated. In a posting on the Sportscard Guaranty's message board, Brian Dwyer, formerly of SGC, confirmed, "We did in fact reject a number of autographed cards, including the Bowman Chrome Pujols," at a show in Philadelphia.

Chrome's slick production values may enhance the line's appeal, but they're no protection against counterfeiting, and just as with older cards, collectors should purchase with caution. ◀ ◀

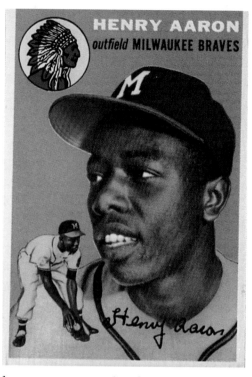

TELLING THE TALE OF HENRY Louis "Hank" Aaron is not as straightforward as it might seem. After all, his success on the field, where he became baseball's all-time home run king, has been clouded by controversy twice.

The first incident occurred on his path to break the home run record. Aaron, who traveled around the major leagues primarily as a member of the Braves organization (spanning its time in both Milwaukee and Atlanta), finished the 1973 season just one home run short of tying the legendary Babe Ruth on the all-time dinger list.

That offseason, Aaron was the subject of numerous death threats and hate mail. The United States of America, at that point, was only beginning to emerge from the cloud of racism that hung over the head of baseball for so many years and relegated so many African American players, including Aaron, to play in the Negro Leagues.

But in the face of pressure and this immeasurable adversity, Aaron excelled, getting the tying home run in his first at-bat of the 1974 season and earning the record just a few days later. There may have been no better signal that Aaron's days of receiving racist threats were over then when two white young men ran onto the field to celebrate Aaron's record-breaking home run, joining him for part of the traditional home run lap. Later that season, Aaron would also break Ruth's all-time runs batted in record and play in his record-tying 21st MLB All-Star game. "Hammering Hank" returned to Milwaukee (as part of the Brewers) later that season to close out his career.

While the first round of controversy was one that Aaron was able to overcome, the second has proven to be damaging to the entire sport of baseball. This one involved Barry Bonds, who, following the 2006 season, was on his way to surpassing Aaron.

That post-season, much like in 1973, anti-record protestors raised their voices; only this time it was because of the perception that Bonds was using performance-enhancing drugs. The rage that surrounded Bonds followed him through and well past the record-breaking home run in 2007, with everyone from fans to card companies (read: Deck, Upper) contributing their potshots.

Aaron fueled the already blazing fires by saying he would not participate in celebrations surrounding the record, though he later clarified his stance by saying it was because he felt records in general should not be celebrated.

As a result of the record-breaking home run, fans have divided themselves between "Team Barry" and "Team Hank," with the result for the collecting world being increased attention on one Henry Aaron, especially on his rookie card. Though Aaron certainly has his share of autograph and memorabilia cards on the market, his vintage cards find their way onto a lot of want lists. The card, which appeared in the 1954 Topps series (not the 1953 Archives series issued in 1991, which included a "what if" card of Aaron), was one of the first sports sets to feature two photos on the front of a card, and while its mustard-yellow background is garish and certainly dumpster-worthy, it actually makes the photos stand out pretty well.

The set's design has been used a few times since this initial release, including in its own reprint series issued by Topps in the early '90s, in future baseball sets and even a WWE wrestling series.

Through it all, Aaron has remained the focal point of the set, as "Hammering Hank" continues to be one of the most celebrated players of all time. ◄ ◄

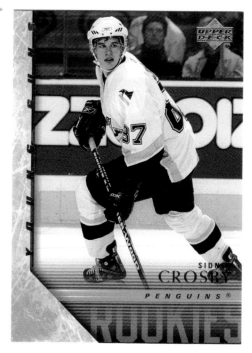

IN 2005, HOCKEY WAS PRE-paring to come back from the NHL's only full-season work stoppage. After own-ers locked players out after what some call the year that saved the sport, shinny was set to return in a big way for the 2005–06 season. Many superstars from the past were either retired or on their last legs and a new generation of marquee names was set to take center stage as the NHL returned to active play.

But it wasn't established veterans like Joe Thornton, Jarome Iginla and Martin Brodeur who would lead the way, it was the single most impressive rookie crop that any sport has ever seen that would take fans on their backs and carry them through the most eagerly anticipated season in decades.

Among these rookies were names that had already gained prominence for either their junior or national play, including Alexander Ovechkin, Dion Phaneuf, Henrik Lundqvist, Ryan Getzlaf and Jeff Carter. But the biggest name of them all, the teenager that the entire league put all its hope in, was Sidney Crosby. Considered to be the next Wayne Gretzky, El Sid was a prodigy from Cole Harbour, Nova Scotia. He had starred in the Quebec Major Junior Hockey League with the Rimouski Oceanic and been a dominant force on Team Canada at the 2005 World Junior Hockey Championships by the time the NHL and its Players Association signed its new collective

bargaining agreement. The NHL also announced that a lottery would take place, giving each team an opportunity (determined by their previous performance) at the number one player in the draft.

The winning team turned out to be the Pittsburgh Penguins. Already having drafter Marc-André Fleury and Evgeni Malkin, the Pens, led by returning captain and owner Mario Lemieux, were primed to make Crosby the NHL's newest hero.

Crosby responded in fine form, leading the Pens with the first of many 100-plus point seasons. Though Ovechkin would beat him for the Calder Memorial Trophy as rookie of the year, Crosby would become the poster boy for hockey.

Of course, by this time Crosby was already a well-known name in the hobby. An In The Game contract, along with Rimouski team issues, meant that dozens of Crosby cards were widely available. All that was missing was an NHL rookie card.

Thanks to Upper Deck, which by this time was the sole licensee for NHL/PA cards, collectors had a variety of cards to pursue, but there were two that dominated want lists and eBay pickups.

The first was the fabled Young Gun card. The subset was already one of UD's hottest properties thanks to years of producing RCs of the game's hottest stars, dating back to Pavel Bure and Sergei Fedorov and more recently including Marián Gáborík and Ilya Kovalchuk.

The Series One set included Crosby's first pack-pulled official NHL card. Despite a print run that ensured every hobbyist could get a Crosby Young Gun (or a dozen), collectors swarmed to pick up the card. It would become the most sought after item at that year's Toronto Fall Expo, the single largest card show in hockey-mad Canada.

Then came the deluge of other longstanding sets. Some collectors would pursue each RC, while others went to their favorites. Crosby was even included in the 2005–06 McDonald's set, creating controversy, as some, including famed price guide Beckett, labeled the food premium as an RC (a big no-no in most collectors' eyes).

As the season progressed, however, word began to leak about a brand new product from Upper Deck — The Cup. Slated to be the most expensive ever produced for shinny, The Cup came in a keeper presentation tin, with cards hand-collated and packaged at the UD factory. Autographs, jerseys, cut signatures, printing plates . . . you name it, The Cup would have it. And all it cost was about $350 — for a tin that usually housed seven cards.

As if the drawing price wasn't promising enough, collectors would soon learn that the Crosby and other top-flight rookies, which included an autograph and a patch (many of which were photoshoot swatches), would be limited to just 99 copies. The game, as they say, was on: the card would reach five-digit sales on eBay and at other auctions.

Both the Young Gun and Cup RCs have since remained the top cards of the NHL's new era. ◀ ◀

El Sid, the cover boy: Crosby checks out Canadian Sports Collector *prior to the World Junior Hockey Championships in 2005.*

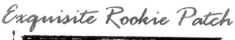

Exquisite Rookie Patch

LEBRON JAMES · CAVALIERS

LEVEL 1   10/99

2003-04 EXQUISITE COLLECTION

TO SAY THAT LEBRON James was at the peak of his collecting popularity when his rookie cards started coming out of packs would surprise some collectors. After all, most players, especially those who go on to have careers as strong as James's has been, would tend to see an increase in interest for their cards.

Not with LeBron though. By the time his rookie cards were issued in the 2003–04 season, there was so much hype surrounding "King James" that anything less than an MVP and NBA championship in his first year would be considered a failure. Heck, if he didn't win the Rookie of the Year award, collectors were sure to declare him the next Bryant "Big Country" Reeves.

For those who weren't fans of the NBA in the years before James's arrival, he was a high school marvel who was destined to skip college and go straight to the NBA. He even had cards from SA-GE, Topps and Upper Deck before he had his high school diploma (though in all fairness, a few companies made cards featuring highschoolers, but that was, after all, the '90s). He had national attention as well — he was a regular on sports highlight reels and his games were occasionally broadcast on pay-per-view or ESPN.

Of course, it certainly helped that the NBA was in desperate need of a new superstar. Michael Jordan's return to basketball with the Washington Wizards wasn't generating the payday that many hoped, and the Shaq and Kobe show in Los Angeles (back when the two were playing nice) was drawing all the excitement. Sure, there were other players collecting oohs and ahhs, but it was nothing like when Larry Bird, Magic Johnson, Jordan and company had been running the floor.

So when LeBron arrived, he had already raised the NBA's profile and established his hobby presence. By the time he played in his first game, he was the single hottest commodity in all of sports. All that collectors had to do now was wait to see how many cards would feature James and pick their favorites.

And with three licensees at that point — Topps, Fleer and Upper Deck — collectors had opportunity after opportunity to pick up King James's RCs in abundance. Every type of card that a company could come up with was packed out. Autographs, jerseys, low-prints . . . you name it, it was available.

But the big surprise was still to come by the time the All-Star break rolled around. At that point, there had been murmurs that Upper Deck was planning something big — something unprecedented for the end of the basketball season, which was normally the cut-off point for cards not considered part of the next year's lineup.

Everyone was blown away when word came that a new set would make its debut: the Exquisite Collection.

Previously, Upper Deck had its Ultimate Collection that packed out well over $100. Exquisite was going to be priced around $500. That's right — half a grand for a pack (actually a wooden box) of five cards. The rookies, including LeBron's, were numbered to just 99 copies each and featured an autograph and a swatch from a jersey patch. The concept may have seemed crazy — to pay that much for so little — but having a solid chance at getting LeBron or one of the other hot rookies (like Carmelo Anthony and Dwayne Wade) or one of three dual Logomen (the NBA logo cut from jerseys) that had the swatches from two of James, Kobe Bryant and Michael Jordan (each of which was a one-of-a-kind card) made the price tag more palatable.

Obviously, LeBron has gone on to be everything most scouts hoped he'd be — an MVP, an endorsement wunderkind and ultimately the face of the league. It's inevitable that he will get an NBA Championship ring as well and will likely go on to have one of the most storied careers in NBA history. ◀ ◀

Had it not been for LeBron, and other current superstars like Kobe Bryant, basketball cards might be harder to find.

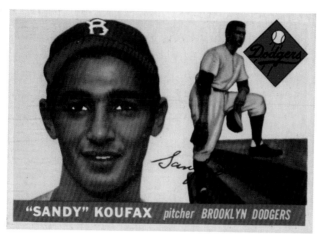

"SANDY" KOUFAX *pitcher BROOKLYN DODGERS*

THOUGH SANDY Koufax broke several major league records in his short career, to his fans, his most important contribution was demonstrating the unquestionable dominance of a Jewish athlete. Koufax, widely regarded as the greatest Jewish player in the history of sport, was a spectacular ball hurler for the Los Angeles Dodgers and the perfect player to get hot for the freshly relocated team.

Koufax made his big league debut in 1955, after tryouts with the New York Giants and Pittsburgh Pirates. His first start was less than impressive — a four and a half inning effort that included eight walks. Just short of two months later though, in his next trip to the mound, he pitched a complete game, two-hit shutout — a teaser of what was to come in one of the greatest, short-spurt, blazing careers in sport history.

Yes, it was just a six-year stint of glory that made Koufax an idol to so many boys and girls across the U.S. It all began in the 1959 season, just a couple years after the hurler started the last-ever game for the Brooklyn Dodgers. Koufax, who had flirted with greatness before, gave fans a new reason for cheering and great expectations as he set a National League record with 18 strikeouts in a single game (a feat that has since been bested by Kerry Wood).

Koufax's career would finally solidify in 1961; he went 18–13, topping Christy Mathewson's NL record for strikeouts in a season, 269–267. (Koufax would later best his own record.) He also played in that year's All-Star festivities, which at the time involved two games. Koufax would follow up with the first of his longstanding record five no-hitters a year later, and in 1963 won the pitching Triple Crown (wins, strikeouts and ERA leader).

But his defining year would be 1965. Though he was already suffering from what would later be career-ending arm trouble, he would again win the pitching Triple Crown, break his own strikeout record and garner his second unanimously selected Cy Young Award. The World Series, however, would be where Koufax truly became a hero. In game one of the championship, Koufax was slated to start — but he refused to play because it was the Jewish high holiday, Yom Kippur.

That moment, according to Martin Abramowitz, the man behind the Jewish Major Leaguers card sets, solidified Koufax's legendary status. "Koufax's decision to sit out Yom Kippur was a huge identity and pride boost to the American Jewish community," Abramowitz said.

Sandy Koufax would go on to pitch two shutouts in the Series, including a game seven championship-deciding gem. His work on the mound garnered him his second MVP award.

After the 1965 season, Koufax's career seemed in jeopardy — and it was. Arthritis was quickly taking over, and 1966 would be his final year in baseball. He would go 27–9, leading the Dodgers back to the World Series, but the team was swept in four games.

With all of these credentials, you'd expect Koufax would have become one of the most in-demand legends on the autograph circuit, and that he would have appeared at many shows and private signings. Koufax, however, shied away from the hobby spotlight, making very few ventures into the memorabilia world until recently. (He signed an agreement with Upper Deck in 2007.)

This reluctance, Abramowitz commented, would lead to a dichotomy in his collectability. "Koufax's absence from the public eye has been a double-edged sword," he said. "It's both added to his mystique, particularly among older fans, and detracted from his potential significance to a younger generation of fans."

Through it all, Koufax's rookie card has remained desirable by fans of all ages, Jewish and otherwise, and will continue to be for years to come. ◀ ◀

IN 1990, PUT- ting a certi-
fied autograph card into a pack was something that most manufacturers had not considered. Upper Deck changed everything
when they inserted a special Reggie Jackson card in their High
Series baseball release.

Known far and wide as "Mr. October," Jackson was a World
Series hero and one of the most feared hitters of the '70s and
'80s. Only three years removed from the game, he still held
some cachet with fans. Upper Deck was well aware of this and
created their first Heroes insert cards to pay tribute to his amazing career. In order to deliver more value in packs, there was
an autographed version of the checklist made available with a
different hologram than on the unsigned card. Limited to 2,500
copies, at the time it was one of the most limited cards on the
market — for any sport — and it changed the hobby forever.

While it wasn't the first certified autograph card to be issued
by a card company, it is certainly one of the most significant and
is still highly sought-after by collectors. The first was actually
a Pete Rose card in a specialty set produced by Topps in 1986,
but it's a card without a huge following; many collectors are
simply unaware of its existence. But after the success of Upper
Deck's Reggie Jackson auto in 1990, every major trading card
manufacturer has inserted a certified autograph card of some
kind into packs and they have become a hobby staple.

The relationship between Jackson and Upper Deck was
fruitful in the company's early years, and they used the former
slugger in both baseball products and a very odd release called

Comic Ball that depicted athletes with *Looney Tunes* characters. In 1997, Jackson would sue Upper Deck for failure to pay part of his contract from 1993 to 1996, but their differences were settled, and in recent years he has once again appeared on their cards.

Like many of the higher-end cards from the boom era, this one lost a great deal of its luster as time passed. It was once a difficult card to obtain, but as many "retired" collectors liquidate their overproduction era cards, more and more turn up. Today it's much more affordable than it was 15 or 20 years ago. There are only a handful of cards that truly changed the landscape of the hobby, and this autograph is certainly among the most revolutionary.

As for the Heroes concept, the moniker existed for a couple more seasons. In 1991, Nolan Ryan and Hank Aaron became the subjects of the set, while Ted Williams was honored in 1992 (before starting his own baseball card company), and the Heroes name would also be used in Upper Deck's other sports series. The insert brand, however, did not survive the bust that followed the boom. Amid increasing demand for other sets and true chases like autograph and game-used cards, the Heroes insert was shelved.

Over a decade later, however, the brand would be resurrected in baseball and football as a full-fledged set. This time, the cards featured past and present players and became a decent hit. The brand would also return to its insert roots in hockey.

For both set and player, the echo era of the hobby has been a blessing, as Reggie Jackson and Heroes maintain good standing among collectors, while the original autograph stands the test of time as one of the most beloved in all of baseball. ◀◀◀

1986 DONRUSS
JOSÉ CANSECO

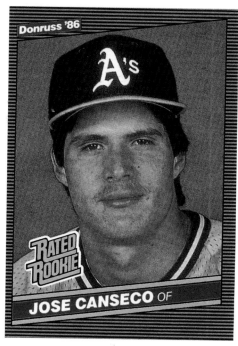

Donruss '86

RATED ROOKIE

JOSE CANSECO OF

IN STARK CONTRAST TO fellow Bash Brother Mark McGwire, who despite using enhancers is still somewhat revered by the hobby, José Canseco has been absolutely vilified both by card collectors and sports fans.

The former darling of the hobby shop has seemingly irreparably tarnished his legacy. After witch-hunting fellow major leaguers in the performance-enhancement drug scandal of the mid- to late 2000s, Canseco has fallen out of favor with his former peers, and he's now become more of a circus sideshow than what a man with his credentials should be.

In his prime, no one equaled José's ability to draw a crowd. For a brief period between 1986 and 1989 (before the arrival of Ken Griffey Jr.), Canseco was baseball's marquee man, after slugging 33 home runs and 117 runs batted in during his first season helped him garner American League Rookie of the Year honors. The arrival of Mark McGwire in 1987 cemented the power hitter as one of the most important and feared roles in baseball.

However, 1988 would prove to be the pinnacle of Canseco's career. That season he became the first player in big league history to hit 40 home runs and collect 40 stolen bases in the same campaign. Add to that a .307 batting average, 120 runs scored and 124 RBIs and it's no surprise that Canseco was named the AL MVP.

One year later, Mighty José's ascension stalled a bit. A wrist injury kept him out of action for the majority of the season, though he was able to come back in time to help the Oakland Athletics to the World Series title.

The timing couldn't have been better for a player who arguably benefited as much, if not more than anyone else, from the rise of the hobby. Canseco's rookies, of which there were many, were hot list regulars despite his injury. He was perceived as a baseball god, so much so that his twin brother, Ozzie Canseco, was able to sponge off the glory and gain some notoriety when his cards debuted in 1989.

As a new decade dawned, Canseco could do no wrong, swatting 37 homers in 1990 and 44 in 1991. Though he didn't reach the 50 home run plateau, many speculated that Roger Maris's 61 home run record was in jeopardy. They couldn't have been further off base: in 1992, the wheels fell off.

Canseco was dealt to the Texas Rangers that year — midgame. What ensued was a kind of tragicomedy. Early in the 1993 season, the now infamous "header" home run occurred: Carlos Martinez hit a ball deep to centerfield, which proceeded to bounce off Canseco's noggin and into the bleachers. But no one was laughing later that same week when Canseco requested to be put in as a pitcher during an insurmountable loss to the Red Sox and proceeded to injure his arm. He was done for the season.

Though Canseco would achieve a couple of flashes of brilliance in subsequent years, including two more 30+ home run seasons, his marquee status was effectively gone for good. Rookie cards that were showcase gems were practically common bin fodder by the time he hung up his cleats in 2001.

A few years later, in 2005, Canseco was back in the news—though not for reasons some may have hoped. Instead of being a potential Hall of Famer, Canseco admitted to steroid use. In his book, *Juiced,* he also named several other players, including Juan González, Iván Rodríguez, Rafael Palmeiro and fellow Bash Brother McGwire as users. The controversy that ensued would lead to Canseco only receiving 1.1 percent of the HoF votes, not enough for his name to stay on the ballot.

His baseball career long behind him, Canseco would look for other opportunities to get in the public eye, appearing on *The Surreal Life* and competing in both boxing and mixed martial arts.

Through it all, the Donruss card has remained the most popular of his rookies, perhaps because of a simple yet attractive design and its relative scarcity when compared to his others from Fleer, Topps and Sportflics. It may never again reach the levels it achieved in the boom era, but that flash of hobby brilliance, for some collectors, is enough to garner a retro demand and earn a spot on our list. ◀ ◀ ◀

José Canseco was one of the featured superstars of another hot trend in the hobby's boom era — Starting Lineups, which gave collectors both cards and figurines.

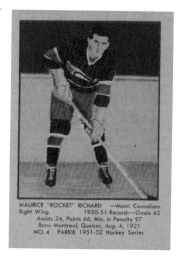

MAURICE "ROCKET" RICHARD —Mont. Canadiens
Right Wing. 1950-51 Record:—Goals 42
Assists 24, Points 66, Min. in Penalty 97
Born: Montreal, Quebec, Aug. 4, 1921
NO. 4 PARKIE 1951-52 Hockey Series

FOR THE PEOPLE OF QUEBEC, THERE IS perhaps no more beloved native son than Maurice Richard. He starred for the Montreal Canadiens from 1942 to 1960, and his impact on Quebec's unique culture is monumental.

Born in Montreal in 1921, Richard was a junior hockey star who worked hard to crack the roster of the Canadiens for the 1942–43 season, but he suffered a broken leg as a rookie. Many thought it would end his promising career, but he came back with a fervor the next year and helped the club to its first Stanley Cup championship since the 1929–30 campaign. He would accomplish an even greater feat in 1944–45 as he became the first player to score 50 goals in an NHL season, reaching the plateau in an astonishing 50 games.

Kids across Canada began to regard Richard as an idol, and he was the topic of many conversations on both the schoolyard and on the ice. Years later, he would inspire Roch Carrier's children's story *The Hockey Sweater*, and it has become a beloved part of the Canadian cultural fabric. It was not until the 1951–52 season that kids had a chance to collect trading cards of their hero, when the Toronto-based Parkhurst Products launched a successful 105-card effort that had all of the league's top stars.

The small cards are primitive by today's standards, but the set features rookie cards of numerous Hall of Famers. It's a challenging collection to put together. The general reaction to the product was sensational and the company would continue to release cards, with only one exception, until the 1963–64 campaign. Every one of those sets would feature members of the

Canadiens and Richard was a part of them until his retirement.

How much the people of Quebec loved and respected Richard cannot be underestimated. After earning a lengthy suspension for his actions during a game in 1955, mobs of fans took to the streets and rioted. Approximately $500,000 dollars in damage was done to the area near the Montreal Forum. The next day, Richard pleaded for calm, but the event is often considered the birthplace of modern Quebec nationalism and the start of the province's Quiet Revolution.

Richard's rookie card features a black-and-white photo taken by the Turofsky brothers (who shot at Toronto's Maple Leaf Gardens) that was tinted with basic skin tones and team colors. It isn't the most attractive of trading card sets, but it has a charm that makes it appealing to collectors even to this day. Copies of any card in this set are tough to find in high grades due to the poor card stock, basic cutting methods (many cards are off-sized) and the fact that the manufacturer shuffled them in a cement mixer and placed them in packs by hand! It is amazing that some of these cards survive in anything close to a high grade, and they can reach serious dollars when offered for sale. ◀◀◀

ON FIRST
glance
there's nothing, to be blunt, especially memorable about the
1953 Bowman baseball series. By this time Topps had established its dominance in the card collecting world. Just a couple
years later it would not only fully affirm its reign, but buy out
its lone competitor. Ask any collector to pick between two cards
of the same player, one a Bowman and one a Topps, and almost
every time they'll gravitate to the Topps issue.

What Bowman did in 1953, however, was create some
absolutely beautiful cards that used, virtually for the first time,
full color photography. Up to that point, cards had primarily
featured black-and-white photography or an artist's color renderings of player images.

But it was this set, perhaps more than any other, that
launched trading cards into the world of vivid color photography, and no card captured the new technology quite like the
one depicting the diminutive Pee Wee Reese.

Harold Henry Reese, nicknamed "Pee Wee" early in childhood, was originally recruited as a shortstop by the Boston Red
Sox, but his arrival to the team was sabotaged by Joe Cronin,
who played the same position. Cronin was sent to scout Reese
while he was playing in Louisville and, fearful of losing his
spot, reported back that Reese wasn't all that he had been
reported to be. In the end, Reese was dealt to "Dem Bums,"
the Brooklyn Dodgers, for four players and cash. One can only
wonder if the Curse of the Bambino would have been lifted
sooner had Reese stayed in Beantown.

Reese went on to have a sparkling career in the majors. Though a broken heel shortened his rookie year, he had already hinted at the promise he would later fulfill. Just two seasons later, he was an All-Star for the first of 10 consecutive seasons — a string that would only be interrupted by three years of military service.

Reese was also the captain of the Dodgers, a role he took very seriously. This was never more evident than when Jackie Robinson arrived. Though Reese was still serving in the military when Jackie was signed, it was Pee Wee who was most instrumental in making him feel welcome. Reese refused to sign a player petition against Robinson being part of the team, and when Robinson was heckled by Cincinnati Reds, it was Reese who famously supported him. A sculpture of the two stands today in Brooklyn.

One has to wonder, though, if the 1953 Bowman card would still have an audience if it was another shortstop captured in its magnificent photo. Certainly, Reese helps buoy the card's popularity and he probably ensured that more copies were kept than discarded. Yet, almost independently of the player, the card stands on its own. The set was one of very few ever produced as a true picture card series. Sure, design elements were relatively unobtrusive in several other series (like Bowman or Parkhurst products that featured only a player's name or signature, or the overproduced Pro Set Platinum series that only carried the brand's logo) but almost no other set features a full, unmodified photo.

Now, years after his passing, Reese continues to be a prominent player in trading card releases. We can only hope that the 1953 Pee Wee card will be officially reprinted in the near future so that more collectors can enjoy it. ◀ ◀

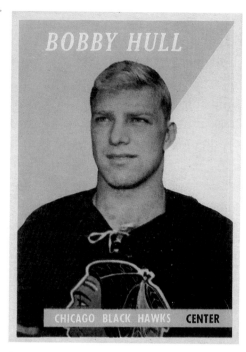

THERE ARE PLAYERS WHO scored more goals and raised more championship trophies than Bobby Hull, but, like Mickey Mantle in baseball, in hockey no one had the charisma or a following like the Golden Jet.

Hull had it all — a powerful shot that would ignite audiences across North America and around the world (as we'd see during the 1976 Canada Cup tournament and other international play), movie-star looks that would increase female audiences at games and flowing blond hair (at least in his pre-toupee days) that made it look like a jet stream trailed him as he glided up and down rinks with ease.

In short, Hull was a star attraction — the kind who drew an audience to the arena and made them stay when they saw just how powerful he was on the ice. He was a Stanley Cup winner, a scoring champion and an MVP. He pretty much did everything imaginable . . . including walking away from the big league to join up with a group of rebels.

Yes, long after his rookie card was issued, Hull left the NHL to join the new World Hockey Association, signing a then-unprecedented $1,000,000 contract to play for the Winnipeg Jets. The move gave the new league instant credibility and, at least for a little while, a fighting chance against the much larger NHL.

Of course, like so many other rebel leagues (some of which

we spotlight elsewhere in this book), the WHA ended up imploding and being absorbed by the NHL. Hull would finish his career alongside another all-time great, Gordie Howe, with the Hartford Whalers.

Had it not been for this amazing career, Hull's rookie card would not be as popular as it is, that's a given. But had it not been for its position in the set, a good condition sample would not be so hard to find.

You see, Hull's card was the last in the 1958–59 Topps series, and in those long-ago days, before plastic holders ensured a card's protection, rubber bands and shoeboxes were the primary method of card storage, meaning that the first and last cards in the series were most susceptible to damage. Thus, if you have a Hull (or any first or last card for that matter) in half decent condition, a-grading you will go. Centering is also a major problem with this issue and that should be taken into account as well.

Since his retirement, Hull has been one of the most visible personalities in the hobby. As the boom era began, Hull became the star attraction of the Ultimate Original Six series, which included autographed cards featuring the Golden Jet and several other NHL legends. Hull would also be featured on promotional cards by Action Packed (though full sets were never produced), and he was recognized in Canadian department store Zellers' series called Masters of Hockey. Later, Hull would appear on cards from Upper Deck, In The Game, Fleer, Pacific, Topps and Starting Lineup (through their various action figure/card combination releases), be commemorated by McFarlane Toys and the Highland Mint series, be featured on a Canada Post stamp and collectible series . . . yeah, you get the picture.

Here's the bottom line — Bobby Hull is probably the most hobby-friendly guy in today's market. Whether you see him at a show, catch him at a hockey game or see him simply enjoying a cigar, Hull always has a smile on his face and a welcome greeting for a fan.

Those factors have made Hull's RC one of the most desirable in hockey history and unquestionably one of the greatest of all time. ◄◄◄

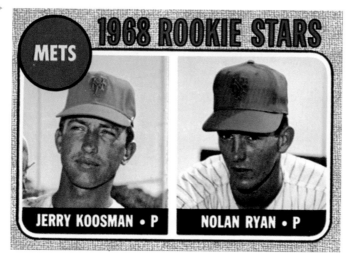

FOR MOST OF the 1960s, the New York Mets were a hard-luck club; they were beloved by fans but had limited success on the field. The team would eventually build itself into a contender, and part of its nucleus of young stars were a pair of pitchers named Jerry Koosman and Nolan Ryan. While the players are forever tied together as a result of their team connection, Topps strengthened the bond by having them appear on the same rookie subset card in their 1968 baseball set.

While not a terribly scarce item since it was in one of the early series that Topps released that year, the card itself is often tough to find in top condition due to its colored borders. There are also some interesting variations of the card that savvy collectors go to great lengths to acquire. One carbon copy of the card was released in a baseball board game by Milton Bradley in 1968, and in Canada, the O-Pee-Chee Company produced part of the set for their market and it is much scarcer than the American version. Even tougher to find is the Topps Venezuelan card that was printed on lower quality cardboard and often pasted into albums by children. Many of these cards that do come up for sale have damage on the back.

Looking at Ryan's statistics, few can doubt his contributions to the game. In 27 seasons, he won 324 contests and holds the all-time record of 5,714 strikeouts. He is a member of the Baseball Hall of Fame and threw an incredible seven no-hitters. He was the game's elder statesman when the trading card industry was entering its boom years and was highly collected. As his legend grew, companies found any possible excuse to put him on cardboard and the public ate it up with great gusto. Values rose — especially for his vintage cards.

Ryan is the real superstar on this card — no doubt about it — but Koosman is no slouch. He would go on to play for three other teams before retiring in 1985 and won 222 career games. Even if he had been paired with a lesser-known pitcher, his pasteboard would still be sought after by collectors. But sadly, his accomplishments became merely a footnote because of the man he shares the card with. The reality is that many regard this as being Ryan's card and its monetary value will forever be tied to his presence.

Had this book been written 20 years ago, this card would be considered one of the best in the hobby, and even though its value has become somewhat stagnant, it still holds a place of prominence for many. What drove the price to unreal heights was the fact that Ryan continued to build on his strikeout record. A true hobby superstar during the boom years, everybody wanted this card, and while it is still desirable, there is a natural decrease or plateau in card values for many players as they are inducted into their sport's Hall of Fame. Ryan is certainly no exception and his (and Koosman's) rookie card now only fetches $500, about half of its heyday price. ◀ ◀

1933 GOUDEY
NAPOLÉON LAJOIE

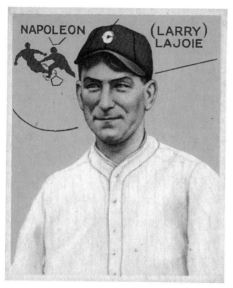

THE IDEA OF A STICK OF bubblegum in a package of trading cards seems both romantic and old-school today, in the aftermath of the boom years. In 1933, however, it was a brand-new concept. For baseball card collectors, it goes back to that first Goudey set. It was a beautiful 240-card collection, loaded with the biggest names in the sport at the time. . . . Or was it?

For kids spending a hard-earned penny on a pack of cards and a slab of gum, or saving up to try to put the set together, there was a problem: card number 106 was nowhere to be found.

This is where things start to get fuzzy. There are some theories why the 1933 release was missing this number. Goudey could have chosen not to print the card as a sly means of selling more packs, creating an endless market of unsatisfied rabid collectors. But it's likely that no one knew who they were looking for — and it is entirely possible that a player may have been cut from the set at the last minute if there was a problem with obtaining the rights to use his likeness.

Regardless of the reason for the card's absence, one of the hobby's earliest pioneers, Jefferson Burdick, is reported to have started a letter-writing campaign to Goudey in order to get the company to rectify the issue. As a result, the company would print a card, depicting retired legend Napoléon "Larry" Lajoie, using the all-new 1934 design but with a back like the 1933 cards. It was sent out to any collector who had written to request it, along with a formal letter of apology. Some hobby historians have casually estimated that only 600 of these cards were released, but there is no proof to back up the claim.

Interestingly, many of the cards that have been uncovered by collectors are in better shape than other 1933 Goudey cards due to the fact that they were less handled and not distributed in the traditional manner.

Lajoie was one of the greatest second basemen in the early part of the 20th century and rose to stardom with the American League's Cleveland franchise. He arrived there in 1902 after a few seasons with the Philadelphia Phillies and Athletics. He gave the club the shot in the arm it desperately needed and they were renamed the "Naps" in his honor. A three-time batting champion, he had a fierce rivalry with Ty Cobb and would retire in 1916 before being elected to the Baseball Hall of Fame in 1937.

As new generations of collectors began to chase the card, it became one of the hobby's holy grails from the pre–World War II era, behind perhaps only the T206 Honus Wagner. While many modern hobbyists have never heard of the card, or of Lajoie for that matter, it will forever hold an esteemed place in the collecting community. Graded copies regularly sell for $25,000 at auction — a good price for a card that almost never existed. ◀◀◀

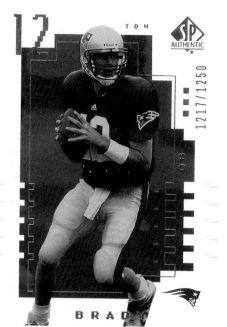

SOMETIMES, IN THE MIDST OF a legendary player's career, you can't truly appreciate their greatness. Sometimes an athelete's career has to end before the masses truly understand their talent.

That may very well be the case with Tom Brady. The New England Patriots gunslinger has been one of the most consistent and popular players in the NFL, and his dedication to the game and straightforward approach to each contest is indicative of the squeaky-clean image he has maintained throughout his career. Yet it wasn't until Brady broke a once seemingly unassailable milestone that he really started to get mainstream collector attention.

Tom Brady has almost always been a name in the football card market. Where so many other players have had up and down seasons throughout their careers, Brady has been a model of consistency since taking his first NFL snap. His early career perfect playoff record, which led his New England Patriots to two Super Bowl titles, got him a lot of press coverage, but he did not have the crossover appeal to fans of other teams like Dan Marino, Joe Montana or even Peyton Manning.

Until 2007, that is, when he really took off. Any talk about his early success being a fluke was forever silenced when he went after two hallowed standards: the record for passing the most touchdowns in a single season and a perfect campaign

— something that had not been done since the 1972 Miami Dolphins.

Both pursuits captured fans and non-fans alike, much in the same way Mark McGwire's and Sammy Sosa's homerun chase captivated a nation. In this case, the Brady-led Patriots were on their way to immortality, while the QB himself reached the magical 50-touchdown watermark, something no quarterback — not Marino, Montana or Manning — had been able to achieve.

Eventually, Brady (who was also named NFL MVP) and company fell just short of perfection, losing a heartbreaking Super Bowl contest to the New York Giants in 2008. The result of that game, however, was almost secondary for a growing base of Brady's faithful: they had already anointed him one of the great athletes of the generation. Of course, this was old news to football card collectors, who were more than happy to tantalize new fans as they boarded the bandwagon. These old hands were like street sellers, playing up to tourists as they passed through the land of gridiron, and their wares were plentiful, with enough variety to turn an observer quickly into a customer.

Like others who have debuted in the last 20 years, Brady has a slew of rookie cards, and while we talk elsewhere about the allure of SP Authentic, the really interesting part of this card is that Brady is not wearing an NFL game jersey. Instead, he's in the Patriots practice jersey, a true rarity in today's sports card market. ◀ ◀

LIKE THE ATHLETES IT PROMOTES, Topps's mantra seems to be "If at first you don't succeed, try, try again." This becomes particularly apparent when you consider the company's relationship with the NBA. While Topps first made basketball cards in the 1957–58 season, it was over a decade before they re-entered that market with some test issues in the late 1960s.

Something must have clicked; they began producing cards for the sport during the 1969–70 season with a 99-card oversized effort that proved to be very popular with young Americans. They'd experimented with the "tall boy" trading card format for their 1965 hockey and football releases, but the size didn't really lend itself to those sports. It also proved confusing for collectors who had become used to the standard 2 ½" x 3 ½" trading card size. For basketball, however, it worked — maybe because of the height of the players — and the company generated enough sales to want to produce basketball cards on an ongoing basis.

Topps also showed great foresight in including a hot young rookie named Lew Alcindor in the set. He was just beginning his amazing professional career: a high school and college standout, there was a lot of interest in his talents heading into the 1969–70 season. At the time, the sport was experiencing an epic battle between the NBA and the ABA, a rival league that was taking basketball to new markets and competing for players with the established loop. Despite a significant offer to play for the touring Harlem Globetrotters club, Alcindor chose to sign with the Milwaukee Bucks (he spurned the New York Nets as well) and was named the NBA's Rookie of the Year after leading his team to a second-place finish in the Eastern Division.

After leading the Bucks to an NBA title as a sophomore, he announced that he would be adopting the Muslim name of Kareem Abdul-Jabbar. On June 16, 1975, he was traded to the Los Angeles Lakers, and his fame grew even greater as a result. Over the course of 14 seasons on the West Coast, he would play for four championship clubs and was consistently one of the league's most popular and visible players. He retired in 1989 and would later be enshrined in the Basketball Hall of Fame.

In the end, the Alcindor rookie card is one of basketball's most iconic first-year pieces. It signaled the beginning of that segment of the hobby being taken seriously by a manufacturer, though hobbyists as a whole would take many more years to begin accepting basketball cards. As the 1990s dawned, Abdul-Jabbar's reputation was reaching legendary status and there was major interest in all of his cards — particularly the one issued for 1969–70 season. Over time, the demand for the card has softened slightly, but that doesn't take away from its position as one of the best in the hobby. ◄ ◄

SPORT KINGS GUM

RED GRANGE

THE 1920S ARE OFTEN REFERRED to as the Golden Age of Sports — people throughout North America began to put aside the bitterness from World War I and looked toward the sporting world as a means of escape.

In football, one of the biggest heroes of them all was a running back named Harold Edward "Red" Grange. Grange was a collegiate star at the University of Illinois before joining the pro ranks with the Chicago Bears barnstorming team in 1925. He was paid the then-amazing sum of $100,000 to appear in 19 games, but after a pay dispute, left to form the American Football League as a rival to the NFL. Though the league lasted just a single season, and Grange briefly stepped away from the game in 1928, the running back would soon return to the Chicago roster. He led the Bears to consecutive championships in 1932 and 1933 before retiring at the end of the 1934 season.

The peak of Grange's career also coincided with the arrival of the bubblegum trading card. Kids everywhere were using their spare pocket change to pick up pictures of their heroes, and the Goudey Gum Company was raking in the profits with their popular sets. One of these collections was an assortment of stars from various pastimes entitled Sports Kings. Made up of 48 cards, Grange was a natural for the set due to his prominence, and collectors consider this card to be his rookie issue.

Many argue that Sports Kings is among the most beautiful trading card sets ever made, and its uniqueness helps ensure its popularity to this day. Though several sets before it covered multiple pursuits, primarily those that were issued via cigarette companies, none covered the world of athletics like Sports Kings. In addition to having cards of elite superstars from the "big four" sports, the set also features elite personalities from swimming, cycling, skiing, skating, horse racing, tennis, golf, boating and wrestling. Truly, only the best of the best were included in this small issue.

Today, the spirit of the Sports Kings brand lives on with a premium trading card product released by Sportkings LP. Featuring players from every major sport, it has proven to be popular with many collectors and is a fitting homage to the original product.

Original Sports Kings cards are highly prized hobby treasures, and any of them is a wonderful addition to a collection. The Grange card stands out in particular as it predates the release of the first recognized football card release, the 1935 National Chicle, by two years, and because Grange was not a part of that series. A charter member of the Pro Football Hall of Fame, his cards and memorabilia will always be collected and competition for them can often be stiff. ◄ ◄

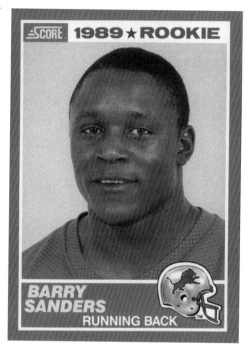

FOR TWO DECADES, TOPPS essentially had a stranglehold on the football card market. But the hobby began to change in 1989 as new manufacturers entered the game. One of those new companies was Score, which had already made a splash with baseball card collectors; its debut football release still ranks among the most popular in the hobby.

What made this set so special? It was a combination of having what was perceived as the smallest print run of the sets released that year and the foresight to create a subset featuring all of the top rookies for the 1989 campaign. It didn't have a huge following at first — the tradition behind Topps and the promotion of Pro Set ranked them ahead — but it carved out a niche and dealers, speculators and collectors jumped on the bandwagon once word started to get around that finding Score wasn't as easy as finding the others.

The 330-card color-bordered set also had the distinct advantage of featuring rookie stars Barry Sanders of the Detroit Lions and Troy Aikman of the Dallas Cowboys. While Aikman's card comes later in our top 100, both were firsts in the market. In fact, the popularity of these rookies practically forced Pro Set and Topps to create update sets to capitalize on these athletes' popularity. In reality, the Score rookie subset cards weren't the most attractive — the subset relied heavily on studio headshots and had garish green borders — but collectors didn't seem to mind in the least.

Sanders made an immediate impact with the Lions and was named the NFL's Offensive Rookie of the Year in 1989. During his 10 seasons, he was a rushing machine: he never dipped below 1,100 yards per year and was named a First Team All-Pro on six occasions. In 1997, he rushed for an incredible 2,053 yards, but he was becoming frustrated by the futility of the Lions. In 1999, he announced his retirement via a fax to his hometown newspaper, and while fans held out hope that he would come back to the game, the return never materialized.

The Score brand still lives today. Produced by the folks at Panini, it has an important place in the hobby as an entry-level brand targeted at young collectors.

As for the Sanders rookie card, it doesn't seem like it will have any sort of major spike in price in the future, but it could enjoy some slow growth should the hobby become more mainstream. Graded copies do sell well, and it is advised that collectors unfamiliar with the regular set purchase a graded card to ensure that they do not end up with a counterfeit copy. ◀ ◀

2000–01 BE A PLAYER MEMORABILIA GEORGES VÉZINA PAD

IN 2000, COLLECTORS WERE BECOMING accustomed to the idea of having a piece of an athlete's game-used memorabilia inserted into a card, but controversy would strike when upstart hockey card manufacturer In The Game announced that they were cutting a pair of goalie pads worn by the legendary Georges Vézina for inclusion in their 2000–01 Be A Player Memorabilia Series release.

Vézina was a goaltender with the Montreal Canadiens from the 1910–11 to 1925–26 seasons. One of the greatest players from that era, he contracted tuberculosis and died during that last campaign. The team would donate a trophy in his name that has honored netminders ever since.

It wasn't the first time that the company cut up a major piece of hockey history as they had memorabilia cards featuring a game-worn jersey from Gordie Howe in their 1998–99 products. But the Vézina pads were the only ones known to exist and hockey historians were up in arms, wondering why someone would destroy something so significant — but their cries weren't heeded. At the time, ITG President Dr. Brian Price spoke with *Beckett Hockey Monthly* and explained his position. "I'm sure some people will say, 'How can you do such a thing?' but I don't follow that logic," said Price. "I'm as much of a collector, a lover of old hockey as the next guy. This is about sharing the piece with fans around the world. If I bought these pads and put them in my collection at my cottage, who's gonna see them? And the average collector couldn't possibly buy something like this. This way, hundreds of people get to share in the thrill of owning something worn by Vézina."

The reality is that Price and In The Game purchased the pads directly from a collector who was aware of the fact that they were being used to be cut up into cards. Despite the uproar from some members of the collecting community, in the same *Beckett* article Price explained how the players and their families feel about collectibles related to their careers. "You'd be surprised how blasé most older players and their families are about their memorabilia," he said. "It's not a big thing to them. They don't see the significance."

In The Game made 16 different cards for the 2000–01 release that featured a piece of the pads. On 15 of them, Vézina was depicted in the background with a player who had won the trophy bearing his name over the previous number of seasons. The final card in the set featured the late goaltender on his own. It's the one that collectors want the most, and it has a book value of $1,000 compared to the $300 to $500 range of the others.

Since the Vézina cards were first released, pieces of his game-used skates and a game-used stick have also found their way into In The Game's products. The furor has died down for the most part, and the company has made inserts from several other historical pieces of memorabilia from numerous Hall of Famers. ◀◀

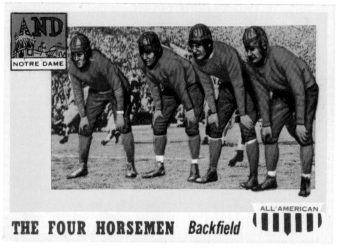

THE FOUR HORSEMEN *Backfield*

IN THE 1990s, Draft Pick and Prospect sets became all the rage for companies like Score Board and Signature Rookies. Unable to secure major league licenses, these companies would rely on college and other amateur leagues to allow them to produce cards for the masses. The plan wasn't bad — the promise of early cards of the likes of Kobe Bryant was enough for them to stay in business for a couple years (albeit not much longer than that).

These series were not, however, the first to spotlight the non-pros. In fact, the early roots of most cards can be traced back to university series, primarily featuring commemorations of schools across the U.S.

In 1955, however, Topps took these cards out of cigarette packs and put them into collector packages for kids. Known as Topps All-American, the set featured the greatest collegiate players in the nation. It has gained a legendary following, in large part due to a deceptively simple and absolutely beautiful design. But the real heat on this set can be attributed to a superior player selection. Many of football's legends are in here, including Otto Graham, Red Grange and uber-athlete Jim Thorpe.

Yet it can be argued that no card has a bigger following than that of the Four Horsemen. No, this isn't the men of the Apocalypse or the NWA wrestlers — in this case the term refers to four Notre Dame players: Harry Stuhldreher, Don Miller, Jim Crowley and Elmer Layden, who were a dominant force for Knute Rockne's Fighting Irish in the 1920s.

The legendary moniker came from Grantland Rice, one of the best sports journalists of his era. In describing a game between the Irish and the Army football teams for the *New York Herald Tribune* on October 18, 1924, Rice wrote: "Outlined against a blue-gray October sky the Four Horsemen rode again. In dramatic lore they are known as famine, pestilence, destruction and death. These are only aliases. Their real names are: Stuhldreher, Miller, Crowley and Layden. They formed the crest of the South Bend cyclone before which another fighting Army team was swept over the precipice at the Polo Grounds this afternoon as 55,000 spectators peered down upon the bewildering panorama spread out upon the green plain below."

The moniker stood throughout the rest of their careers, and they would later be photographed atop horses in a famous picture orchestrated by student journalist George Strickler. Some 70 years later, the photo was immortalized on a stamp issued by the U.S. Postal Service.

Curiously, not all four players would suit up in the big leagues. Only Layden and Stuhldreher would play pro football — they would team up for the Brooklyn Horsemen, named in their honor. The team played only four games in the AFL before merging with the Brooklyn Lions and being absorbed into the rival NFL. Only Stuhldreher played for this new team.

All four, however, would be associated with football in one way or another after their college days. They all became coaches and Layden eventually served as NFL commissioner.

With this history, it's somewhat surprising that more cards weren't created of the legendary collegiate heroes. The first was a Notre Dame postcard in 1924 and the most recent was part of the famous Sportscaster series issued in 1978 and 1979. Of the handful of cards available, however, none has reached the legendary status of this Topps card, arguably the most popular in the series. ◄ ◄

THE HOT-
test goalie in hockey in the mid-1950s, Jacques Plante starred for the Montreal Canadiens, and when his rookie card was released during the 1955–56 season, he was in the midst of backstopping the legendary franchise to the first of what would eventually be five consecutive Stanley Cup championships.

Interestingly, Plante's rookie card is not the first time he appeared on cardboard — he was featured on several action cards in the previous year's release. However, subset cards aren't usually called rookie cards in vintage sets, and he would first receive a full card to himself in 1955–56. The card depicts a wonderful game action shot, and it was an instant hit with Canadian youth. It was also the first set that Parkhurst created that just featured the Canadian NHL teams since the cost of doing business with the clubs had gone up dramatically.

Due to the tremendous interest in hockey cards in Canada at the time, the Quaker Oats company decided to partner up with Parkhurst and make a parallel version of their set to help sell boxes of cereal. To differentiate the cards from each other, the Quaker Oats cards feature green ink on the back instead of red and do not have a trivia question. The promotion was heavily advertised, but the green-backed cards are incredibly rare today, since many were likely destroyed when they were redeemed for prizes that could be obtained when you finished the various subsets. Those that completed the entire 79-card set, for example, would receive a bicycle; those completing the set of current Maple Leafs or Canadiens obtained a pair of skates. Even those who accumulated any 20 cards could send them in for a felt crest.

The 1955–56 Parkhurst and Quaker Oats cards can be a real source of frustration for collectors looking to put together a set in high grade condition. The main problem (outside of frequent miscuts or poor centering) is the fact that the red area that holds the player information on the front often wears so that yellow ink shows through. The odd set size of 79 cards may also cause a number of short or double prints to exist, but until a full uncut sheet appears on the collector's market, it will be impossible to determine if some cards are more scarce than others. The Quaker Oats set is even crazier to collect: there are four cards that are considered impossible to find.

Plante became the first NHL goaltender to regularly don a mask during gameplay and stayed with the Canadiens until the end of the 1962–63 season. He spent some time with the New York Rangers and stepped away from the game briefly before returning to action with the St. Louis Blues in 1968–69. He would eventually finish his career as a member of the World Hockey Association's Edmonton Oilers during the 1974–75 season. A true innovator, he later became a member of the Hockey Hall of Fame. Plante died in 1986.

No matter which version of his rookie card collectors attempt to obtain, they are spending their money wisely. The Quaker Oats card commands a hefty premium and requires a greater effort to track down. ◀ ◀

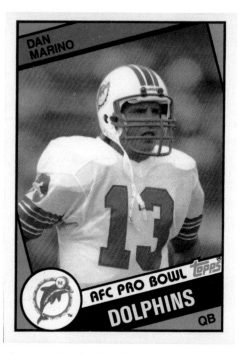

NO MATTER WHICH SPORT you follow, there's always a lovable loser who pops up among the elite — the player who had a fantastic career but was never able to win the big game.

In hockey it's Marcel Dionne, who finished his career as the NHL's second-leading goal scorer but never won the Stanley Cup. In baseball, it's, well, anyone who played for the Chicago Cubs. In tennis, there's Anna Kournikova. . . . Okay, that's a bit of a stretch, but you get the picture.

There is perhaps no one as equal in individual greatness as he is in team ineptitude as Dan Marino. The Hall of Famer turned broadcaster and occasional actor (*Ace Ventura*, anyone?) was as good as any quarterback in pigskin history, yet the Vince Lombardi Trophy forever eluded him.

It's hard to say what it was that was missing from those great Dolphin teams. True, Marino didn't have a superstar receiver like Joe Montana had in Jerry Rice, a legendary defender like Brett Favre did in Reggie White or an uber-threat running back like Troy Aikman had in Emmitt Smith, but Marino was still the true definition of "quarterback." He was the undisputed leader of his team from his first snap to his final throw, and he probably shouldered more of the blame for seasons that, every year, began with great expectations but never delivered the prize.

That's not to say that the Dolphins were sadsacks under

Marino's leadership. Quite the contrary, under number 13's missile-like guidance, the Fish made the playoffs 10 of 17 times. Marino set QB records in the process, many of which are still intact, including most passing yards in a season (5,084) and most games with 300+ yards passing in a career (63).

The card we've selected from Marino's illustrious list of pieces may actually surprise some veteran collectors. After all, between signatures, jerseys and ultra limited inserts (and base cards for that matter), there are some cards that are more valuable.

But there's only one card that every Marino fan should have, and it's this release from Topps.

The card is hardly the only highlight RC from the set. Howie Long, Jackie Slater, Roger Craig, Morten Anderson and the legendary Eric Dickerson are all in this landmark series, but it is only Marino's career-long rival, John Elway, who even comes close to competing for the most prized card spot. The two had legendary battles on the gridiron, and to this day, fans still have heated debates over who was the better gunslinger.

Topps also ensured that collectors had plenty of options when it came to getting cards from Marino's first year. Along with the rookie card is an Instant Replay subset card, a League Leader dual with Steve Bartkowski, a piece in the Glossy insert series and two pieces in the Topps Sticker set from that same year. Marino also made a cameo appearance on a second Instant Replay card. Marino's true RC, however, stands above all the others and will, inevitably, stand the test of time. ◀◀◀

1963-64 PARKHURST
GORDIE HOWE

THE 1963-64 SEASON SIGNALED THE END OF AN era for hockey card collectors: it marked the final time that Parkhurst released a set. The company had been around since the 1951–52 season; over the course of its history, the way it produced trading cards had changed dramatically, but it was still focused on the main goal of selling gum to the masses.

Since 1960–61, Parkhurst was focused on making hockey cards from just three of the NHL teams from the era — the Montreal Canadiens, the Toronto Maple Leafs and the Detroit Red Wings. It worked well since they were essentially the most popular and successful clubs of the time, but the rights to depict the players were starting to become expensive. Regardless, for the 1963–64 season they would put together their biggest set in years at 99 cards and most of the Toronto and Montreal players would receive two cards each. Maple Leafs were depicted in front of the pre–maple leaf Canadian flag, while Canadiens stars were placed in front of a background that featured brightly colored horizontal lines.

The Detroit players, on the other hand, were all placed in front of an American flag, and the result was pure magic. Each card looked amazing and there was none better than that of club leader Gordie Howe. At the time, he was in his 18th NHL season and had recently become the league's all-time leader in goals when he surpassed Maurice Richard's career total of 544. Even though he was the game's elder statesman, he was showing no signs of slowing down after winning his sixth scoring title in 1962–63.

Parkhurst was on its last legs as a hockey card producer in 1964 due to spiraling costs. While their demise allowed Topps to take over the market, in 1991 the company would resurface under Dr. Brian Price as a premium brand distributed by Pro Set. After two seasons, in 1993–94, the brand was moved to Upper Deck, and Price would release future products on his own for the next two seasons. With the 50th anniversary of the first Parkie set in 2001, In The Game would release a cross-brand collection that paved the way for more successful releases. Upper Deck acquired the rights to the brand name in 2005–06 but only issued two products before it was placed in creative limbo. The name is sure to return at some point in the future, but only time will tell how it will be used.

For its sheer attractiveness, the 1963–64 Parkhurst Gordie Howe will always be chased by collectors who want to own something truly special. A true hobby treasure, it may not see wild price fluctuations, but high-grade versions will always command a healthy premium. Not every collector wants to shell out the few hundred dollars for one of these cards, but luckily, authorized reprints were done in the early 1990s when Parkhurst was relaunched. ◀◀

THE 1996 NBA DRAFT WAS loaded with players who would make an immediate impact on the game and eventually become superstars. Allen Iverson went first overall to the Philadelphia 76ers and he would be followed by big names like Stephon Marbury, Ray Allen, Peja Stojakovic, Steve Nash and Jermaine O'Neal. However, one name would be bigger than them all — a prodigy named Kobe Bryant who was selected by the Los Angeles Lakers.

It was rare at the time: Bryant was plucked straight from high school, rather than going the college route. (Okay, it's not an everyday occurrence even now.) Such a move was a risky venture, but if ever a highschooler was a sure thing, it was Bryant.

When the 1996–97 season was finally in full swing, Bryant was among the hottest players in the hobby. He was the youngest NBA starter ever and would win the 1997 Slam Dunk Contest. More and more that year, collectors tried to hoard his cards from any of the multitude of products that were on the market at that time.

The best of the cards would prove to be the result of an interesting experiment by Topps. They took their regular basketball set and printed the cards on foil stock using technology that they had been employing on their Finest products since 1993. Topps Chrome had what everyone wanted at the time. It was limited, had lots of rookies in the 220-card set, and used foil stock. With a combination like that, they couldn't go wrong. Considered to be a condition-sensitive set, highly graded copies of this card can go for serious dollars and are tough to find.

Produced exclusively for the retail market, hobby shops did whatever they could to get the four-card packs of Chrome in stock and sold them well above their suggested price of $2.99 . . . if they could get them at all. To top it all off, there were also Refractor versions (cards that, when held at an angle, have a rainbow shimmer) of the base cards that created a frenzy for any of the key rookie and star cards. The Chrome experiment proved to be a boon for Topps, as it took the format into other sports and non-sports releases with a great deal of success. It has been a staple for the company for over a decade and should continue to be for many years to come.

With each of Bryant's many accomplishments, his Chrome rookie card would see increased demand. A four-time NBA champion, he would later sign an exclusive autograph deal with Upper Deck, but that would end in 2009 when the NBA license was exclusively taken over by Panini. Bryant is already regarded as a sure-fire future Hall of Fame member, and this card may eventually prove to be the quintessential basketball card from the 1990s. ◀◀

TOP 10 BLUNDERS BY SPORTS CARD COMPANIES

SURE, WE LOVE THE HOBBY as much as anyone else, but there are just some ideas that were epic failures. Here are our 10 favorite bloopers and blunders from the world of cardboard.

1 ▶ COMIC BALL

Right smack in the middle of the era when cards were aimed at adults came this kid-themed set that paired *Looney Tunes* and baseball's greats like Nolan Ryan. Suffice it to say, the set was as lame as any product that has hit the market in the past 50 years. Sufferin' succotash!

2 ▶ ARENA ROOKIES

What is a company to do when they can't get licensing from any leagues? Some will choose to stage their own game for a photo shoot (Ultimate Draft Picks hockey) while others will take the road far less traveled — putting their players in tuxedos. We're guessing Arena doled out more cash for the rentals than they made selling these sets.

3 ▶ 1991 SCORE JOSÉ CANSECO DREAM TEAM

Was Score trying to lure in female collectors with this card? We're not sure, but a shirtless, black-and-white shot of José Canseco wasn't appealing to many male collectors. Maybe putting players in tuxedos wasn't a bad idea after all.

4 ▶ 2001 TOPPS XFL

Even long after the boom era was dead, it seemed as though any sports league that showed half-assed signs of life would land a trading card contract. That's exactly what the XFL got when it signed on with Topps. The 100-card base set was complemented by jersey cards of "stars" such as Chuck Clements.

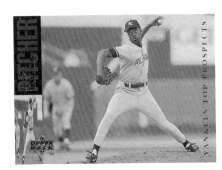

5 ▶ BRIEN TAYLOR

Draft picks are always a crap shoot for a pro sports team — and for card companies as well. After all, for every Peyton Manning there's a Ryan Leaf. The biggest blunder was when companies went hog wild for Brien Taylor, a New York Yankees draftee. Taylor didn't even make it to the big leagues.

6 ▶ 2001–02 UPPER DECK INSPIRATIONS LIL' BOW WOW DUAL JERSEYS

What inspired the good people at Upper Deck to make cards of rapper Lil' Bow Wow is beyond us. What made them create cards that featured the tyke's jersey from *Like Mike* as a dual with players like Allen Iverson is even more of a mystery.

7 ▶ 2002–03 BOWMAN YOUNGSTARS JEREMY WALSH "RC"

Collectors on cards? It happened in 2003 in Bowman hockey. Topps commemorated NHL All-Star Game towel boy Jeremy Walsh on a card that should've just been given to his family rather than being packed out. Worse, Topps repeated this blunder in 2009 when they produced cards of a contest winner from the previous year for "cracking the code," a sleuthing contest that asked collectors to decipher symbols on cards in the Allen and Ginter set.

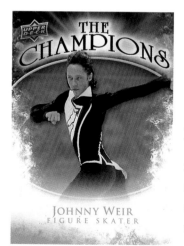

8 ▶ 2009–10 UPPER DECK THE CHAMPIONS JOHNNY WEIR

If there are two sports that don't mix it's hockey and figure skating (despite what fans of *The Cutting Edge* or *Battle of the Blades* think), but that didn't stop Upper Deck from producing this card as part of an Olympic tribute series. Collectors can also hunt (if they choose to) for an autographed version.

9 ▶ 2003 TOPPS
BRANDON PUFFER/JUNG BONG

Do we need to spell out the reason why this card is on the list? Someone at Topps either has a sense of humor or, how shall we say, was in an altered state when they put this rookie duo together. Oh, it's funny . . . but others may not see it that way.

10 ▶ PRESS PASS SKID MARKS

Cool concept — using race-used tires as part of the printing process — but horrid execution on the name of this set. If there's ever been a card set that has had a worse name, we'd like to hear an argument for it. . . . Wait, maybe not . . . ◀◀◀

51 TO **75**

1951–52 PARKHURST
"THE WINNING GOAL"

THE WINNING GOAL   April 21, 1951
Barilko scores against McNeil, bringing the
Stanley Cup to the Toronto Maple Leafs
for 1950-51.
No. 52 in the "PARKIE" 1951-52 Hockey Series.

A PHOTOGRAPH IS FOUND ON VIRTUALLY every card ever created, but this all-important element is often taken for granted. Too frequently, collectors will pass over what are at times spectacular photos or renderings in favor of a name or a serial number, ignoring the simple beauty of a card. This kind of error could very well have meant that cards like this would be overlooked.

The year was 1951, and Parkhurst debuted with mini art pieces dedicated to the top players of the day, some of whom are featured elsewhere in this list. There was one card made differently than all others, however, and it featured Bill Barilko's historic Stanley Cup–winning goal.

It wasn't the first hockey "action" card, but almost everything before and after it pales in comparison. The paint job, which at times was cruel to this series, looks spectacular. And more importantly, the photo captures a moment unlike any other. Compare it to the variety of cards featuring Bobby Orr's or Alex Ovechkin's version of "The Goal" — they just don't measure up. When you factor in the passing of six decades, the achievement is all the more remarkable.

The story of the man behind the goal has turned what may have been an otherwise small tale into the stuff of hockey legend. The summer following the Toronto Maple Leafs' 1951 Stanley Cup victory, Barilko went missing during a fishing trip. It was more than a decade until his body was discovered. Coincidentally, it was the same year that the Leafs next won Lord Stanley's mug: 1962.

The loss of Barilko was tragic. Beyond being a hero in the '51 series, he was an extremely popular and talented player. "Bill was fun loving, a real prankster who kept the mood light in the dressing room," said biographer Kevin Shea. "He loved the outdoors, although he hated eating the fish he caught, and hanging out with friends back home in Timmins [Ontario]."

Though the story of his mysterious death kept Barilko in the minds of hockey fans of his generation, it might have disappeared amidst the Gen X and Y card collectors, had it not been for Lud Denny and his company, Pro Set, which in 1991–92 included a card of Barilko and his famous goal in its Hall of Fame subset. So beautiful was this new card that it would inspire Tragically Hip frontman Gord Downie to write the band's hit "Fifty-Mission Cap" and bring Barilko's tale back to life. "The card that inspired The Tragically Hip brought Bill's story to a generation that would never know anything about a player who otherwise would have been long forgotten," Shea said.

Despite specifically mentioning the card, The Tragically Hip song didn't immediately inspire a rush of sales. In fact, it wasn't until years later, when Dr. Brian Price's In The Game Inc. began producing new Barilko cards in the 2003–04 series Parkhurst Original Six and 2004–05 Franchises that the Pro Set card really began to create a buzz.

Why? Well, despite the naming of the card, the Pro Set piece had not been labeled as an RC by the hobby media, much like its Parkhurst predecessor. So, there was some debate as to the true rookie card, which sent collectors scurrying to find the Pro Set card, instantly making it the most desired non-insert in the history of the company.

The debate over the Pro Set and ITG cards would also renew interest in the original Parkie, which, outside of cut autographs and some memorabilia cards, remains the most cherished card of the tragic hero.

That debate continues, but in Shea's eyes, the original Parkie, the Pro Set card and those that have followed have only benefited one of the most unique men in NHL history. "Bill's legacy has been kept alive through the memories evoked by his hockey cards," Shea remarked. "The goal, arguably the most famous in Maple Leaf history, has made the tragic story of this young Leaf hero all the more poignant." ◀ ◀ ◀

1993 SP
DEREK JETER

52

New York Yankees

FOR ANY CARD COLLECTOR WHO questions why so many different rookie cards are produced every year, there's a simple two-word response: Derek Jeter.

Before the New York Yankees became the multi-billion dollar juggernaut that appeared in the playoffs on a regular basis and were expected to challenge for, if not take, the World Series year-in and year-out, the club was a mere shadow of its glorious self. In the early 1990s, the Yankees were in a desperate search for the next marquee name. Don Mattingly's career was starting to wind down, Rickey Henderson had returned to Oakland and Dave Winfield was already a distant memory.

The 1992 MLB Entry Draft was the scene: Jeter, surprisingly passed up by five other teams, was taken sixth overall. Back then, Derek Jeter was, well, let's say . . . not the kind of player you'd pick out of a crowd of prospects as baseball's next big hobby superstar.

"He was a skinny infield prospect on a club that hadn't won a lot of playoff games prior to his arrival. He had little hype when his cards came out in 1993," said Grant Sandground, Upper Deck's baseball product development manager.

A funny thing happed though — the skinny infield prospect debuted just a couple years later and would end up usurping Tony Fernandez as the Yankees shortstop by the start of the 1996 season. Joe Torre's gamble paid off, as Jeter hit .314 and had 78 RBIs, propelling him to the American League's Rookie of the Year award. The team would go on to win the World Series that year.

Jeter would become the pride of the Yankees for the next decade and a half, accumulating five Golden Gloves, four Silver Sluggers, 11 All-Star appearances, five team MVP honors, a World Series MVP award, five World Series championships, one Hank Aaron Award (top hitter) and numerous other accolades. But all that success comes with a hobby industry caveat. Several other stars have had similar track records in smaller markets such as Milwaukee, or with teams that don't have a fan base that's as large (the Florida Marlins, for example), but they aren't held in as high regard — something that Sandground attributes to Jeter being a lifelong member of the Bronx Bombers.

"He would definitely *not* be as highly collected," he said when asked if Jeter would be as popular on a different team. "He's not a big power hitter and much of his popularity is that he's the definitive player, and team captain, on the most important team in the sport."

In much the same way that Jeter had an immediate impact on the Yankees, so too has the SP brand grown in the hobby. When Upper Deck introduced the brand in '93, the two letters were already familiar to fans, usually standing for "single print" or "special print." The call letters evoked a sense of a limited release, something that wasn't seen in most products those days.

Since that first set, a number of other brands have been borne from SP, including SPx, SP Authentic and SP Game Used, but it can be argued that none compare to the original SP branding, from which the best Derek Jeter rookie card emanated. ◀ ◀◀

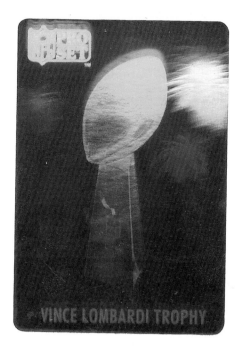

FOR MANY COLLECTORS, the mere mention of Pro Set sends them into a rant about overproduction, errors and lack of quality control. But, despite the bad feelings, the much-maligned company did manage to produce some interesting and appealing cards.

Pro Set was the brainchild of an ambitious fellow named Ludwell Denny. Denny took his love of trading cards to unheard of levels, creating the company that would start out by producing an "official trading card of the NFL" in 1989. That first release was relatively successful: it was the first season that football card collectors finally had an option outside of Topps and a few smaller, regional issues.

A boom began and Pro Set was in the thick of it — but while its products sold fairly well, it also showed some signs of the bad things to come. There were notable errors on cards — misspelled player names, wrong positions listed and the like — and promotional rarities like the card depicting Santa Claus. . . . Still, all things considered, the prognosis for 1990 was good.

Pro Set had a major ace up its sleeve for the first series of that year's football set: it revealed to collectors that there was a chance to pull a limited-edition hologram card depicting the Vince Lombardi Trophy — the award given to the Super Bowl champions. "Only" 10,000 copies were issued, and the hunt was on. Arguably the first true chase card the hobby would see, the resulting mania led to excitement whenever it was pulled. Some unscrupulous types even used a metal detector to attempt to locate one, and others shelled out hundreds of dollars just for the right to say they owned one.

There also appears to be a rare parallel version of the card called the Owner Edition, which has the name of an NFL team owner written in the space that is normally reserved for the serial number. Truly a one-of-a-kind item, a copy intended for former Philadelphia Eagles owner Norman Braman was selling on eBay in 2010 for the bargain price of $149.99.

By 1993, Pro Set's fortunes had taken a turn for the worse and the company filed for bankruptcy. We asked Denny to speak about the company's legacy for this book, but our calls were not returned. It was a wild ride for "the little company that could" but too many negatives contributed to its downfall.

Strangely, in recent years there has been a growing fondness for the Pro Set brand among collectors. The Lombardi Hologram is still a very strong seller. Some of the rarest Pro Set error cards and promotional issues still sell strongly as well and may often rise above book values if more than one collector is competing for them. ◀◀

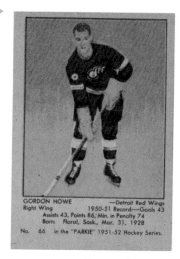

GORDON HOWE —Detroit Red Wings
Right Wing 1950-51 Record:—Goals 43
Assists 43, Points 86; Min. in Penalty 74
Born: Floral, Sask., Mar. 31, 1928
No. 66 in the "PARKIE" 1951-52 Hockey Series.

THE FIRST HOCKEY CARD SET OF THE modern era was issued during the 1951–52 season, and the landmark release contains rookie issues for many members of the Hockey Hall of Fame. But of all the men who have gone on to be enshrined in the hallowed halls, none is greater than Detroit Red Wings legend Gordie Howe.

At the time, Howe was a rugged right winger coming off his first Art Ross Trophy win as the NHL's leading scorer; he was also among the most popular players in the sport. For Canadian youth, the Parkhurst cards were something new and exciting: a nickel gave them a pack of cards and a piece of gum. Howe himself relates to the the experience; he's often reminisced about searching through the back alleys of Saskatoon for Beehive Corn Syrup cans as a youth — he'd collect them for labels he could exchange for premium photos of NHL players the company offered.

Howe first joined the pro ice wars as a teenager during the 1946–47 season and by the dawn of the 1950s he'd developed into one of the game's top offensive stars. Howe won the Art Ross Trophy four consecutive times from 1950–51 to 1953–54 and added two more scoring titles later in his career. A four-time Stanley Cup champion, he would eventually become the league's all-time leader in games played, goals, assists and points over the course of 26 seasons. While he temporarily stepped away from the game in 1971, he would later spend six seasons playing in the World Hockey Association with his sons, Mark and Marty, on the Houston Aeros and New England Whalers. He returned to the NHL with Hartford for a final season at the age of 52 in 1979–80. His on-ice leadership earned him the admiration of millions and cemented his reputation as one of the game's greatest players.

The Howe rookie card has been one of hockey's holy grails for decades and it almost always produces a solid return for those who purchase one as an investment. The card is a strong seller in almost any condition, which means collectors need to keep their eyes open for counterfeits. Official reprints have been issued by the modern Parkhurst company in recent years but they are in the standard card size.

A nicely graded copy of the Howe can command a hefty premium because the 1951–52 collection suffered from registration issues, uneven cuts and was, as we've mentioned, packaged using a crude method that involved pulling the cards out of a cement mixer by hand. That combination made it almost impossible for a collector to pull a truly mint card from a pack even 60 years ago, but nice copies do surface on occasion and command serious money in PSA 8 condition or greater. ◀ ◀

1869 PECK & SNYDER CINCINNATI RED STOCKINGS

EVERY modern sport has its humble beginnings. It takes years, decades, sometimes even centuries for high level competition to fully develop. Rules need to be established and refined, and playing surfaces need to be tweaked. Further, for professional sports, athletes who can play the sport expertly and draw a crowd must be recruited and marketed.

But whether it was basketball, hockey or the American version of football, each had to start somewhere. And for the game of baseball, "somewhere" was Elysian Fields in Hoboken.

It was 1845 when the first game was played. A simple thing, its roots were a ball, a bat, four bases, some fielders, a pitcher and a hitter. As legend has it, the game spread from its northeastern roots during the American Civil War — to the extent that when the war ended, a national pastime was born.

The first professional players would come together in a club known as the Cincinnati Red Stockings. Managed by Harry Wright, the Red Stockings were sponsored by a group of investors, and while the team did not have a true superstar on its roster, the Red Stockings established a precedent for all of sport: paying athletes.

But with baseball's oldest franchise, at least as far as collectors go, the signature accomplishment was not that the Red Stockings made money — it was that they appeared on one of the first cards.

Oversized by today's standards, the Red Stockings card is a singular ad piece (for a New York–based sporting goods company, Peck & Snyder) cleverly disguised as a keepsake of the Cincinnati squad. Like many cigarette, tobacco and chewing gum cards, the intention was likely not to urge children to keep the piece as a memento, but to encourage them to tell their parents of the wonderful cleats, ball gloves and bats they could buy.

Hurley, Sub.; G. Wright, S.S.; Allison, C.; McVey, R. F ; Leonard, L. F. Sweasy, 2d B.; Waterman, 3d B.; H. Wright, C. F.; Brainard, P.; Gould 1st B.

RED STOCKING B. B. CLUB OF CINCINNATI.

According to a February 10, 2009, article on Sports Collectors Daily's website, less than 10 copies are thought to still exist, and the Red Stockings card has now become so rare and valuable, that any time one surfaces, it becomes national news. Such was the case in 2009, when Bernice Gallego uncovered the rare treasure. Though the card initially was placed on eBay, Gallego and her husband Al would eventually bring the card to Memory Lane Inc., which would auction it for more than $75,000. Talk about a treasure in the attic.

Whether or not the original marketing ploy worked is impossible to assess. At the very least, Peck & Snyder continued to operate for another two decades before being purchased by Spalding, a company that continues to be a player in the sporting goods universe. ◀ ◀

Shaquille O'Neal

HEADING INTO THE 1992–93 season, hopes were high for a young rookie out of Louisiana State University named Shaquille O'Neal. He was the first overall choice in the 1992 NBA Draft by the Orlando Magic, and at the age of 20, he seemed to be basketball's next big superstar.

Naturally, collectors were also excited for O'Neal's cardboard debut. But there was a snag: it came in the form of an exclusive deal the big man had with Classic, the company that had him signed until the end of 1992. Classic managed to issue certified autograph cards of O'Neal in its product, and those cards were hugely popular and considered quite limited for the era. This gave Classic a huge advantage over its competition for a couple of months, so NBA-licensed manufacturers had to come up with a way to make their early season products appealing.

Enter Upper Deck with an innovation that forever changed the landscape for collectors — the redemption card. After a solid debut in 1991–92, they were out to make their sophomore effort a good one. The first series packs contained a special card that could be sent in to receive a card of the hobby's hottest young star once his exclusive with Classic had ended. The company also included several other cards to show its appreciation for collectors' patience. For the time, it was a bold move, and it paid off in a big way: the card was one of the hobby's hottest for the remainder of the season. If anything, it had created the greatest buzz for a single basketball card since the release of the Hoops David Robinson produced three years earlier.

Other manufacturers also jumped on the O'Neal bandwagon that year, including Topps, which had just returned to producing NBA cards after an 11-season hiatus. In addition to a regular base card, they also issued a Topps Gold parallel for O'Neal and featured the young rookie in the Stadium Club release, including the tough-to-find Beam Team insert. There was also a redemption card for Shaq found in packs of Hoops, but it does not seem to have the same enduring appeal of the Upper Deck card.

For collectors who chased O'Neal's cards that season, dreams of paying for their children's education with the cards have never even come close to panning out, but they do serve as a reminder of an era when basketball cards moved up to the forefront of the hobby. And the fact remains that O'Neal has had an amazing career, which has included four NBA championships, two scoring titles and a trophy case full of accolades. He's a sure-fire first ballot Hall of Famer, and while his rookie season cards were produced in relatively high quantities to meet public demand, few rookies will ever elicit the same reaction from collectors again. ◄◄

IN THE EARLY 1950S, THE war between Bowman and Topps for baseball card supremacy gave kids throughout America two collecting options, but behind the scenes, Topps was looking to deliver a death blow to their competition.

At the time, players signed individual deals with one of the companies. A star might be found in one product, but be noticeably absent from others. Bowman had a stranglehold on St. Louis Cardinals superstar Stan Musial for many years, and Topps would not see him appear in one of their regular issues until 1958. Bowman also had a deal with Boston Red Sox slugger Ted Williams during the 1950 and 1952 seasons but the ingenuity of hobby icon Sy Berger would change the playing field dramatically after Williams returned from serving in the Korean War.

Berger, a longtime member of the Society for American Baseball Research, recounted the experience for the organization's SABR-Zine in 2004: "Fred Corcoran was Ted Williams' agent, and I told him I had a program I wanted to talk to him about that included Ted. I spoke to him and told him how I would feature Ted and we would do Williams honor. And he got up and he says, 'Kid, I like you. You got Teddy.' And we made a five-year deal. It was exclusive. . . . He could only be on

Topps picture cards for the next five years . . . '54 through '58. And it was only $400 a year. Don't forget that then we paid for exclusive contracts. Bowman was paying $100, we were paying $125 for exclusive, $75 for non-exclusive. And Williams was probably getting $100 from them. This is going back to the old days. Then in '54 Bowman thought they had an option but they didn't and they printed his card, but they could not include it. [Once Bowman printed the card,] we threatened to sue them because we had a contract. Of course some of them got out, but they had to go and hand pick the cards out."

As a result of Topps's brilliant move, Bowman had to replace the Williams card with one featuring his teammate, Jim Piersall. Since Topps had Williams exclusively from 1954 to 1958, collectors were treated with several memorable cards bearing his likeness. In fact, during his first year with the company, he would appear in the set twice, bookending the product, with cards number 1 and 250. Those cards are especially difficult to find in top condition due to the fact that many kids would collate their sets with rubber bands or put them in boxes that would see the first or last cards potentially receive damage from being handled excessively. In 1959, Williams went on to sign an exclusive deal with Fleer for a tribute set after Topps refused to match an offer of $5,000 from their upstart competitor.

While time has proven that the 1954 Bowman Ted Williams card is not as scarce as some collectors would have liked to believe, it is certainly a card steeped in history and has its fair share of collectors trying to track it down. Its significance in the hobby is undeniable, and it should be considered a must-have for vintage card enthusiasts who dabble in baseball collectibles. ◀◀

15. HOWARD MORENZ
CANADIENS · MONTREAL
National Hockey League

HOCKEY HISTORIANS OFTEN MAKE the case that Howie Morenz was the sport's first true superstar. His amazing talents helped open the American market for the fledgling National Hockey League in the 1920s.

Known as the "Stratford Streak," Morenz made the Montreal Canadiens' roster at the beginning of the 1923–24 season after an impressive training camp. His exciting play helped drive the club to a Stanley Cup championship that year. Fans were enthralled with the young star and he quickly became the face of the NHL.

During his rookie campaign, the first set of trading cards featuring NHLers hit the market as the William Patterson Company decided to use pictures of the game's stars to help sell chocolate bars. The Patterson Hockey Bar was an immense hit, partially because it was believed that the black-and-white 40-card set could be redeemed for a pair of skates. In order to reduce the number of prizes awarded, the Bert Corbeau card was seriously short printed and kids everywhere were on the hunt for the elusive number.

The Morenz rookie card was included, alongside a number of other Hall of Famers, like King Clancy and Aurèle Joliat, who were appearing on cards for the first time. Known to most collectors as the V145-1 set (its assigned number from the *American Card Catalog*), the issue is tough to find in top shape because of bad cuts and the fact that sets sent back to the company were likely destroyed. A complete graded set with a Corbeau card that had a hole punched into it as a cancellation came up for sale via Classic Auctions in 2008, selling for $116,203. In 1924–25, Patterson issued a larger set that added players from the expansion team, Boston Bruins. That set has been designated V145-2 due to the similarities between the two.

The 1920s have often been referred to as the "Golden Age of Sports" by historians, and Morenz certainly did his best to raise the profile of hockey in North America. When the New York Americans were set to open their 1925–26 season, they insisted that their first opponents be the Canadiens so they could thrill an audience who had come to see speedy skating and slick offense. The NHL would add another New York–based team the next year, along with franchises in Detroit and Chicago.

The game was looking to expand and a great deal of promotional responsibility was placed on the able shoulders of hockey poster boy Morenz. He would win scoring titles in 1927–28 and 1930–31 and be named a three-time winner of the Hart Trophy as the NHL's most valuable player. After his point production began to falter, he would spend time with the New York Rangers and Chicago Blackhawks before returning to Montreal for the 1936–37 campaign. Sadly, he broke his leg during a game that season and passed away just six weeks later, after suffering a heart attack at the age of 34. The team held a public funeral; thousands of fans packed the Montreal Forum to say goodbye.

As is typical of the sport's early days, there are just a handful of trading cards depicting Morenz to collect. All of them are highly sought-after, solid sellers in any condition. ◀ ◀

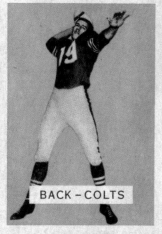

John Unitas

BACK – COLTS

LONG BEFORE Peyton Manning became a god in Indianapolis, there was once a QB who many thought would rank as the best Colts pigskin tosser of all time: Johnny Unitas.

Unitas, known as "The Golden Arm," was in some ways Manning's antithesis. Manning, as we all know, was the number one pick in the 1998 NFL Draft. Unitas, meanwhile, was a ninth-rounder taken by the Pittsburgh Steelers. Thankfully for Colts fans, he never got the opportunity to play behind the Steel Curtain.

Manning has also never had to do anything but play football — well, aside from appearing in commercials and occasionally on shows like *Saturday Night Live*. Unitas had to take a second job while playing semi-pro ball and waiting for his opportunity to play in the big leagues.

Once that opportunity came, Unitas wasn't going to let it slip away. In 1956, he joined the Baltimore Colts. A year later, he was the league's MVP. Not exactly the Curse of the Bambino, but it's safe to say that the Steelers would have been an even more dominant franchise had they kept Unitas in the fold.

Just two years into his NFL career and one into his tenure with the Colts, Unitas would earn his first card, courtesy of Topps. It was a unique year in card design — the company produced what on first glance would seem a dual card, with equal space for a head-and-shoulder posed image and a full-body gunslinger shot (interestingly sans helmet). White borders around each image on the front and the back drew an invisible yet unmistakable "cut here, please" line between statistical information and the always popular Topps cartoons, and, inevitably, some kids cut it in two.

Unitas would also do one thing that Manning is not likely to do — retire with a team other than the Colts. He concluded his playing days with the San Diego Chargers after leading the Colts to a Super Bowl victory.

If there is any commonality between the two men (well, other than wearing the same colors), it is that each player is the seminal quarterback for his respective Colts hometown. The team's move firmly established two eras, each with its lead QB.

Sadly, the second incarnation of the Baltimore Colts city-nickname combination did not last as long as the first. When Baltimore joined the Canadian Football League in 1994, the team was supposed to be called the CFL Colts before an injunction by the NFL led to the team at first being known as the Baltimore Football Club (or more comically in the media as the Baltimore _____), and later as the Baltimore Stallions. This team also enjoyed championship success, becoming the only American franchise to win the Grey Cup. In 1996, the club would move to Montreal, resurrect the Alouettes name, and eventually employ another legendary QB, Anthony Calvillo.

Since his death in 2002, Unitas has remained a popular figure. Cards featuring the Colts legend continue to be issued, including a couple reprints from Topps in recent years, most notably the 2001 Topps Archives series. ◄◄

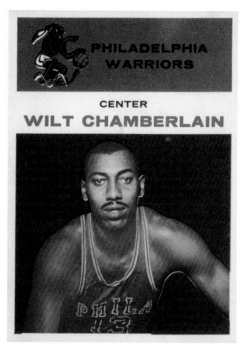

IN THE LATE 1950s AND early 1960s, the hype for a hot NBA rookie was something entirely different than it is today. Had Wilt Chamberlain been in a modern media environment, it is quite possible that his legend would be even greater than it is.

After leaving college early to play the 1958–59 season with the Harlem Globetrotters, he was a territorial pick by the Philadelphia Warriors in the 1959 NBA Draft. In 1959–60, he was the league's Rookie of the Year.

Since basketball cards were a rarity in those days, he would not appear on cardboard until his third pro season. The quirky-looking 1961–62 Fleer set was the third major basketball series to be released, and it featured 66 cards, 22 of which depicted players in game action. The design evokes a much simpler time for both the trading card industry and the NBA. Chamberlain is featured on both a regular card (which is considered to be his rookie issue) and an action card.

In some respects, it was a smart idea to attempt to create a market for basketball cards after Chamberlain set several records as a sophomore in 1960–61. The reality, though, is that the set wasn't a big seller. Fleer would not produce a set featuring NBA players again until its classic 1986–87 collection.

Around the time that his card was released, Chamberlain's legend soared to amazing heights. His most notable solo achievement came on March 2, 1962, when he scored 100 points in a game against the New York Knicks. He would also lead the league in a variety of statistical categories that year.

But all of his hard work on the court that season couldn't save the team. It proved to be the last campaign the Warriors would wage in Philadelphia. They headed to sunny San Francisco for the following season. After a year and a half there, he returned to Philadelphia to play for the 76ers — the team that rose from the ashes of the old Syracuse Nationals and brought roundball back to the City of Brotherly Love.

Chamberlain would not have another major issue card until Topps jumped back into the market during the 1969–70 season, but he continued to be one of basketball's elite superstars and someone who helped the sport reach a wider audience. On four occasions, he was named the NBA's Most Valuable Player, and he played on two championship teams. In retirement, he would become enshrined in the Basketball Hall of Fame and even tried his hand at professional volleyball. He also starred in the 1984 action flick *Conan the Destroyer* with Arnold Schwarzenegger.

Sadly, his greatest contribution to popular culture appears to be the claim that he slept with more than 20,000 women. He made the boast in his autobiography, *A View from Above*, and it took on a life of its own in the sporting and mainstream media. It also came at a time when basketball cards were hot. His vintage releases would quickly become common finds on want lists, and though he passed away in 1999, he did manage to sign trading cards for Upper Deck prior to his death that are extremely popular with collectors. ◀ ◀

1997 UPPER DECK GAME JERSEY KEN GRIFFEY JR.

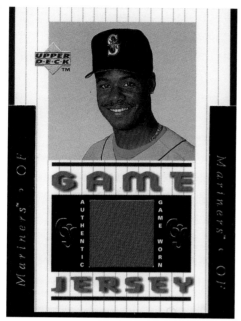

61

IN THE HISTORY OF SPORTS cards, it can be argued that the single greatest innovation was the game jersey card. Think about it — gamer cards were the one piece that had seemed impossible to collectors. Getting cards autographed was not exactly uncommon when the first certified autographs appeared on the market, rookie cards were always deemed special because they were the first of a particular player (even before the designation became a common collector term) and short printed cards had been around since the early days of redemptions.

No, it took a bit of creativity (and guts, as you've read elsewhere in this book) to take a game-used item, cut it up and embed it in cardboard.

But that's exactly what Upper Deck did in 1996 when it created its first Game Used Jersey set as part of its football series. The concept was followed up in other sports, including baseball for the 1997 base brand set.

Inserted at nearly impossible odds by any standard (let alone those of today, when a collector might pull multiple memorabilia cards per pack), the cards launched in the big four sports to high demand, and one of the cards leading the pack was this card featuring Ken Griffey Jr.

Junior, as you may recall, was one of the hottest players in baseball during the recovery period after the strike that canceled the 1994 World Series. His sweet swing was belting out pitches at a pace that many believed would mean he'd surpass

Hank Aaron as the all-time home run king. Add to it that Griffey was one of the most popular players in the game among both the media and fans, and you had the recipe for one of the most in-demand cards of the 1990s.

Following the release of the set, a second run of jersey cards was included in UD's second base brand series.

It's interesting to note, however, that Upper Deck was not the first company to run with the gamer concept. A few months preceding the Upper Deck football release, Racing Champions issued the first-ever memorabilia cards, putting pieces of NASCAR tires into its Press Pass Burning Rubber inset series. Those cards, released in January 1996, didn't seem like a big deal at first, but once UD brought out the Griffey and other ballplayers, the hobby world, starved for an echo after the boom and bust, had its newest sensation.

Since Griffey and co. were the first players to have their jerseys cut, thousands upon thousands of players past, present and yes, even future have had their uniforms and equipment cut up for the sake of memorabilia cards. Virtually everything imaginable, including jerseys, shoes, stadium walls, bleacher sets, tickets and playing surfaces have been sliced up and embedded.

Because it was the first, the Kid Griff Upper Deck 1997 jersey card remains a highly in-demand card and is likely to stay hot for years, especially once Ken Jr. is inducted into baseball's Hall of Fame. ◄ ◄

1984 FLEER UPDATE
ROGER CLEMENS

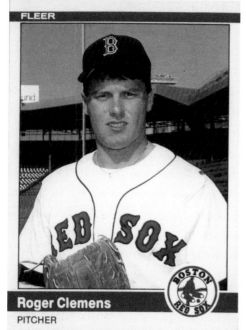

62

FLEER

Roger Clemens
PITCHER

SOMETIMES A PLAYER'S behavior after his professional career ends can have a negative impact on how the public remembers him — as a result, the value of his trading cards and memorabilia begins to decline.

One of the greatest examples of this phenomenon in recent years is Roger Clemens. The Rocket's rookie card has fallen, hard, from its former perch as the most valuable regular issue baseball card of the 1980s.

In 1984, Fleer decided to follow the lead of Topps and offered hobby stores an Update set that featured traded players and the season's hottest rookies. Produced in relatively limited quantities for the era, the boxed set took off in value quickly. Part of the rise came from the presence of two fresh faces the competition ignored — Kirby Puckett of the Minnesota Twins and Roger Clemens of the Boston Red Sox.

Puckett would win a pair of World Series titles and go on to be enshrined in the Baseball Hall of Fame; Clemens was destined for greatness as well. His career really didn't begin to take off until 1986 when he won the first of seven Cy Young Awards and led the Red Sox to the World Series against the New York Mets. (We all know how that series would end.) Clemens would spend 13 seasons with the club, and after two more with the Toronto Blue Jays, he moved to the New York Yankees. With the Bronx Bombers, he was part of three consecutive championship clubs and also became a member of the 300 Win Club.

According to hobby lore, the Fleer Update was limited to 5,000 sets, which seems like a large print run by today's standards, but as the booming baseball card market was soaring to great heights in the mid-1980s, it was miniscule. It was geared toward collectors rather than children, but the set was placed rather tightly into its box, and, as a result, it can often be hard to find high-grade versions of many cards.

Steve Babineau, who shot for Fleer from 1980 to 1994, recalled taking the photo for Clemens' classic card early in the 1984 season: "He walked out of the dugout and I really had no idea who he was at that point. I hadn't seen him pitch and since I was Fleer's set-up pose guy that is how it came about."

In retirement, Clemens' reputation was tainted by controversy. An extramarital affair with country music singer Mindy McCready was revealed. And then came the steroid-use allegations. The media frenzy took over, vilifying him in the eyes of many fans. The already softening demand for his cards was accelerated greatly — to the point that his once-popular rookie card plummeted in value. It's possible that his chances of being elected to the Baseball Hall of Fame may be diminished, but even being immortalized among his peers may not have a positive effect on his card values. ◀ ◀

63

1910–11 C56
CYCLONE TAYLOR

Nº15

FRED. TAYLOR of RENFREW CLUB.

THE EARLY DAYS OF PROFESSIONAL HOCKEY were full of amazing characters and talented players, but few shone more brightly than Fred "Cyclone" Taylor, one of the game's earliest true superstars.

Born in the small town of Tara, Ontario, in 1884, Taylor was one of the first players to declare himself a professional, when in 1906 he played for the Portage Lakers out of Houghton, Michigan. Soon after, he would relocate to Ottawa to play for the Senators club, while also starring on the lacrosse field. He quickly emerged as one of the top offensive powers in hockey and in 1910, the newly formed Renfrew Millionaires signed him to a deal that made him the highest-paid player in professional sports on a per-game basis. One of the greatest stories involving Taylor from this era claims that he skated down the length of the ice backwards and scored a goal. While there is no conclusive proof that the feat actually occurred, the story built his legend and cemented his status as a marquee attraction.

During the 1910–11 season, the first hockey cards became available to the Canadian public and they featured 35 top stars from the National Hockey Association. (The set is actually made up of 36 cards, with Art Ross of Haileybury, Ontario, featured on two pieces.)

The set gives modern fans of the game a glimpse of a simpler time. Many of the game's earliest marquee names and innovators are a part of it, including brothers Frank and Lester Patrick, scoring machine Édouard "Newsy" Lalonde and, of course, Taylor. Some of the featured teams are lost to the mists of time — the Cobalt Silver Kings and the Renfrew Millionaires, for example — but the set does depict original members of the Montreal Canadiens club, wearing blue and white jerseys that were recently resurrected for their centennial season.

The set, which was dubbed C56 in Jefferson Burdick's *American Card Catalog*, was issued in cigarette packages by Montreal-based Imperial Tobacco, and its cards are stylistically similar to the T206 baseball cards issued during the same era. They are also incredibly scarce and collectors go to great lengths to put a set together in any condition.

Taylor would later head out to British Columbia to play in the Pacific Coast Hockey Association that was formed by the Patrick brothers. He starred for the Vancouver Millionaires for many seasons and won a Stanley Cup in 1915. He stepped away from the game in 1923, but remained in the Vancouver area, working as a government official and even running for political office in the early 1950s. An original member of the Hockey Hall of Fame, he was instrumental in helping bring the National Hockey League to Vancouver in 1970 and was an avid supporter of the Canucks. In 1979, he died two weeks before his 95th birthday, and the Canucks honored his memory by naming their Most Valuable Player award after him. ◄ ◄

ONE OF THE MOST INTER-esting trends among basketball collectors recently is a resurgence of interest in some of the more limited insert and parallel cards from the 1990s. Prices for inserts of the legendary Michael Jordan have gone through the roof — some sell for hundreds of dollars. It may be an indication of a new appreciation for cards that have been maligned for years while certified autographs and game-used memorabilia pieces have dominated the marketplace.

Insert cards really aren't a new concept for collectors, as manufacturers had been giving the public something extra in packs for decades; however, as hobbyists cried out for more limited cards to add to their collections, the companies decided to up the ante by seeding certain inserts at varying rates in packages, thus generating more interest and helping spark sales. It was a smart move; completists wanted to get everything they possibly could, and if the insert cards were compelling enough, secondary market sales would explode.

For basketball collectors, the trend hit hard for the 1992–93 season when there seemed to be more sets on the market than ever before. Following more than a decade away from the sport, Topps returned to the hardcourt, and after a successful initial release of their basic set, they decided to unleash the fury of their uber-popular Stadium Club brand that had been a smash hit in other sports mostly due to amazing photography, borderless designs, UV coating and foil stamping. The product had all the bells and whistles needed to cause a buzz — including the presence of the Beam Team insert set that would become a mainstay with the product for years to come.

Topps took some of the game's greatest stars, featured them on a cool design and put them into second series boxes at a rate of 1 in 36 packs. The set is made up of 21 cards, including Jordan and Shaquille O'Neal, who was the hottest player in the hobby at the time. Despite the fact that the design looks somewhat dated, the Jordan card is still a strong seller and a pristine graded copy can sell for as much as $300. There is also some interest in the Members Only parallel version that was reportedly limited to 10,000 copies. These variations were only available to collectors who purchased a Stadium Club membership and took the time to order a set for a nominal fee. A relatively new concept, the Members Only angle would be extended into other sports and created some limited parallels that collectors still actively chase today.

Bigger and flashier insert cards would follow in the coming years and the arrival of autographs and memorabilia would change what collectors wanted to find in packs. For a time, though, the insert card was the king of the hobby, and while it may never return to that lofty perch, there will always be some nostalgia for a time when collecting was a little simpler. ◄ ◄

1948 LEAF
JOE LOUIS

BOXING CARDS HAVE LONG been a subset of the hobby that's ignored by mainstream collectors, despite being around for over 100 years. In fact, some of the earliest trading cards, primarily issued in cigarette packets, were of pugilists.

Part of the reason for the lack of boxing collectors is the fact that the cards are now rarely produced as today's manufacturers are often hesitant to take a risk on a property that has never been effectively tested. However, for those in the know, boxing cards are as great a challenge to collect as any other sport, and it's only a matter of time before they earn some hobby love.

In the late 1940s, a gum manufacturer called Leaf caught the attention of kids with trading card sets featuring baseball and football stars, but they also put out a collection of cards featuring boxers that is incredibly tough to track down today. Like its compatriots, the boxing set (Knock-Out bubblegum) was skip-numbered and is considered complete at 49 cards. There is a 50th card featuring Rocky Graziano that was discovered in the 1990s, but since it is so difficult to find, some collectors theorize that the ultra-short printed card may not have been intended for wide release. Additionally, rumors of other previously uncataloged cards continue to surface.

Like so many sets in the early post-war era, the Leaf cards had a premium offer for kids. In this case, the backs of the cards also offered up a special album that kids could purchase directly from the company for 25 cents. Anyone who finds one of these today in decent condition has a true, and very underappreciated, rarity in their hands.

The real gem in Leaf is the card featuring the legendary Joe Louis. Often considered to be the first African American athlete to become a national hero, he was the World Heavyweight champion for a record 11 years and 10 months from 1937 to 1949 and absolutely dominated the sport. He defended his title on 25 occasions before announcing his retirement on March 1, 1949, with a record of 65–3 with one no contest and over 50 knockouts.

Following his career, Louis received many accolades, but there is perhaps none greater than the honor his home city of Detroit bestowed upon him. In 1979, the city opened a new arena, primarily for use by the Detroit Red Wings NHL team, and paid homage to the legendary boxer by naming it the Joe Louis Arena.

Like the almost unbeatable boxer, the card itself is a tough customer, not just due to scarcity, but also because the set suffers from major color registration issues that can make some copies look terrible.

Over the next few years, the 1949 Leaf Joe Louis will certainly see a steady rise in value due to his impact on pop culture and the overall scarcity of high-grade copies of the card. A resurgence of the card's popularity could also occur thanks to the renewed production of dedicated boxing cards sets from Creative Cardboard Concepts. ◄◄

JULIUS ERVING   FORWARD

THE AMERICAN BASKETBALL Association had a strange and rocky history, but time has shown that fans have a soft spot in their hearts for the players and teams that made up the rebel league from 1967–68 to 1975–76.

The 1972–73 Topps set was the largest basketball issue to have ever been released at the time, containing 264 cards, 88 of which were devoted to the ABA. One of those cards featured a young star named Julius Erving, who was at the beginning of his Hall of Fame career. This was the second year for ABA cards in the set, and for several seasons Topps would include players from both leagues so collectors would be able to get all of the game's biggest stars in a pack of cards. It was odd to see that two rival leagues could cooperate on something like that, but the sport itself was not at a point where either league could really demand exclusivity. In contrast, during the same season, the O-Pee-Chee company in Canada would include cards from both the NHL and the WHA, but there was enough uproar to ensure that the two rival hockey leagues would be featured in separate releases over the next few years.

Since he was not yet eligible for the NBA Draft, Erving signed with the Virginia Squires as a free agent out of the University of Massachusetts prior to the 1971–72 season, and he was named the ABA's Rookie of the Year. He was instantly one of the league's marquee attractions but the Squires had to move him to the

New York Nets in 1973, a move that would propel New York to its first championship. During this time, Erving became the face of the financially troubled league, but even his amazing on-court exploits couldn't save the ABA. The two leagues merged in 1976, and Erving was sold to Philadelphia, where he thrilled crowds with amazing dunks and an NBA title in 1982–83. "Dr. J" would also begin making an indelible impact on pop culture through endorsement deals and film appearances.

Billy Cunningham coached Erving during his time with the 76ers and famously summed up his contributions to the game: "As a basketball player, Julius was the first to actually take the torch and become the spokesman for the NBA. He understood what his role was and how important it was for him to conduct himself as a representative of the league. Julius was the first player I ever remember who transcended sports and was known by one name, Doctor."

As time goes by, the legacy of the ABA continues to shine despite the league's shortcomings. The nostalgia for an era of garish uniforms, sparse crowds and the red, white and blue ball is strong, and Erving is generally considered to be the league's most recognizable talent. His rookie card is one of the most sought-after of its era, and there will always be a strong demand for it as future generations of fans learn about the league and its history. ◀ ◀

1986–87 O-PEE-CHEE PATRICK ROY

HOCKEY CARD COLLECTING was still a youthful pursuit in the mid-1980s, but the boom was around the corner and everything was about to change forever. One of the players who would help the hobby grow was a young goaltender named Patrick Roy, who took the beloved Montreal Canadiens to a Stanley Cup title as a rookie in 1986.

Since that accomplishment was fresh in the minds of fans at the time, Topps and O-Pee-Chee put him in a place of prominence for their 1986–87 product when they placed his card on the front of the box in order to pique the interest of consumers. The card, which features him wearing a white mask that would soon be painted to pay tribute to his club, slowly became one of the hobby's cornerstones heading into the boom years.

In fact, counterfeit versions of this celebrated card have found their way on the market, and buyers need to do their homework in order to avoid getting burned. There are also shady collectors who will take an original wax box from his rookie season and cut out the card depicted on the front in an attempt to sell it as a proof. There also appear to be a large number of blank-backed sheets that have been cut up and sold on the secondary market, also as proofs.

Roy himself was known to be a hockey card collector and his on-ice play certainly helped the card become a must-have.

Many modern goaltenders acknowledge him as a major influence, and his hybrid goaltending style has been adopted by players at all levels. By 1991, he was such a popular player among collectors that he was tapped by manufacturer Pro Set to sign some cards in its first series for the 1991–92 season. It marked the first time that a certified autograph card would be available to hockey card collectors, and it still remains popular to this day.

One year after the Pro Set release, Roy would help the Canadiens to yet another Stanley Cup victory, but he would be traded to the Colorado Avalanche midway through the 1995–96 season. Over the next few years, he would take the Avalanche to a pair of championships and would surpass Terry Sawchuk as the NHL's all-time leader in games played and wins by a goaltender. Roy retired after the 2002–03 campaign and was inducted into the Hockey Hall of Fame in 2006. At present, he serves as coach and owner of the QMJHL's Quebec Remparts.

While Roy's records have since been surpassed by Martin Brodeur of the New Jersey Devils, he is sure to remain one of the most popular players among hockey fans. Some of his rarer cards regularly sell for high prices, and fans are also waiting to see if he will make the move to coaching at the professional level. The legacy he left is impossible to deny and his rookie card is likely to be considered among the hobby's greatest for many years to come. ◀ ◀ ◀

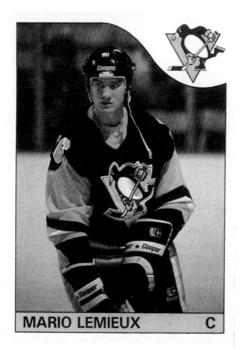

MARIO LEMIEUX   C

SOMETIMES WE HEAR OF A professional athlete being diagnosed with a disease that will, in all likelihood, end their career, or at best sideline them for upwards of a year. Rarely, though, do we hear stories of a player not only returning to his game, but doing so with such assurance that you almost forget that he was even gone.

This was precisely what "The Magnificent One," Mario Lemieux, accomplished.

During the 1992–93 NHL season, Lemieux, riding on the momentum of leading his Pittsburgh Penguins to two Stanley Cup championships, was on top of the league in points and goals, seemingly set to smash single-season records, and his team seemed destined for a three-peat.

Then, in mid-January, Lemieux was diagnosed with Hodgkin's lymphoma. Immediately, Mario took leave from the Penguins for radiation treatment. On the day of his last session, he flew to Philadelphia to rejoin his squad, potting a goal and an assist in his return.

This act of unbelievable resilience and determination was not an isolated one for Lemieux. Throughout his storied career, which included two retirements (one in 1997 and one in 2006), Lemieux battled back injuries and other ailments. Despite these woes, he put together one of the most phenomenal careers in professional sports, winning multiple scoring titles (Art Ross

Trophy), Most Valuable Player honors (Hart Trophy) and other accolades. At the end of that fateful 1992–93 season, Lemieux was named the recipient of the Bill Masterston Memorial Trophy, given to the player annually who best displays perseverance and dedication to the sport.

Lemieux is also the only man in NHL history to score a goal in every possible way (regulation, overtime, penalty shot, short-handed and power play) in a single game and led Canada to the 2002 Olympic gold medal, at the time the hockey-mad country's first in almost 50 years.

He was also, and continues to be, a major name in the hockey hobby. In 1993, the debuting Leaf/Donruss company announced that Lemieux would be one of its spokesmen and he would remain with the company through its eventual sale to Pinnacle Brands.

To this day, Lemieux continues to be a hot name; often at the top of collector want lists, he's a venerable "white whale" for many fans. Over the years, full series have been dedicated to "Super Mario," including subsets, insert series and standalone products. At one point, he even had his own candy bar — the Mario Bun.

But above all others stands this card. Part of a 1985–86 series that is believed to have been produced in much smaller numbers than its predecessor, Lemieux's rookie card was a highlight card in the boom era of the hobby and continues to demand three-figures, despite the sour look on Mario's face.

The card has had up and down periods, but has maintained a level of respectability, as have the other cards issued of Mario that year, including a Topps version, subset cards, a box-bottom card (easily distinguishable because of its yellow borders) and a coveted "credit card" style issue from 7-Eleven convenience stores in Canada. ◀◀

LEROY PAIGE

IN BASEBALL'S LONG HISTORY, there are many inspirational stories — the kind that make you believe, if even just for a few moments, that all is right in the world. But baseball also has an ugly side, one that is filled with the type of tales that would make boys and girls drop their bats and gloves and not want to ever pick them up again.

The one that haunts baseball more than any other is the long, twisted saga of segregation. Major League Baseball, for the better part of its first 80 years of existence, would not allow African American players into its brotherhood. The very idea of black and white ballplayers sharing a field was taboo.

Some, however, will inevitably take the apologist's position, blaming not the game, but saying instead that baseball was only reflective of the segregation that ruled America in general. After all, it wasn't until 1955 that Rosa Parks famously refused to move to the back of her bus.

Seven years before Parks's rebellion came one of the biggest events in Black American history — the integration of base-ball. And while Jackie Robinson was the first African American to crack the lineup of an MLB team, he was hardly the last. He was soon followed by a number of other players, including Leroy "Satchel" Paige.

Paige's story is unique. While popular practice, even in the old days, was for a player to sign with one team and remain with it for a season (or longer as was most often the case), Paige would travel from team to team, working as an independent contractor much the same way a professional wrestler would bounce around from territory to territory. The feature attraction model paid off greatly for Satchel, whose legendary status grew as he went from city to city and country to country (including spending time in Cuba, Puerto Rico and the Dominican Republic), plying his trade for a new set of fans eager to pay big bucks to watch him in action.

But Paige really shone in the Negro Leagues. Despite all his travels, he would have successful runs with Birmingham, Pittsburgh and Kansas City, the last of which he helped lead to a championship.

Eventually though, it came time for Paige to settle down and set up shop with a single Major League ball club — at age 42. Setting a record as the oldest rookie in MLB history, Paige debuted with the Cleveland Indians in July 1948 in a relief role. One week later, he had his first victory under his belt. Very quickly, Paige would turn in record crowds at home and away. One season later, however, Paige's stuff had diminished enough for him to be released.

Despite his limited time with the Indians, it was here that Paige earned his true rookie card. It was issued by Leaf in 1949; the company was one of the top confectionery outfits in the land when it made its breakthrough baseball series, one of the first true card sets ever produced.

Leaf's inaugural run would not last long, and by the time that the Bowman/Topps wars began, Leaf was a distant memory. It would not appear again until the 1980s, when, after a long and complicated series of acquisitions and sales, Leaf purchased the trading card brand Donruss from General Mills. Leaf would first reappear in Canada as the northern equivalent of the popular baseball brand, then later as a premium series. Leaf cards exist today, after another round of corporate takeovers, under the Panini name.

After returning to his barnstorming roots, Paige was signed by the St. Louis Browns and made his mark in the hobby with what is arguably his second most popular card, the 1953 Topps issue. His time in the majors, however, would not be long, and Paige would head to the minors and eventually barnstorm again, well into his sixties.

Today, Paige's rookie card is a treasure for any collector, selling well into five figures. ◄ ◄

1985 TOPPS
MARK MCGWIRE

IN A SET THAT FEATURED the first full release Topps cards (or rookie cards to some) of Dwight Gooden, Kirby Puckett, Roger Clemens and other stars, it was Mark McGwire's that, for years, commanded the most attention. There are two reasons.

First, as mentioned earlier, several of the players already had rookie cards on the market, technically speaking, thanks to the 1980s phenom, the Update set. That set took the form of a boxed series that included players who debuted during a season, rather than highlighting them and their full rookie accomplishments the next year.

McGwire's card, however, was a true rookie card. Not yet the household name he would become as a member of the Bash Brothers, or as the man who broke Roger Maris's home run record and helped saved baseball in the mid- to late 1990s, McGwire was, at this point, a fresh-faced player for Team USA. Commemorated in this release following the 1984 Summer Olympic Games in Los Angeles, McGwire was the lead dog in a group of future pros, including some lesser names like Shane Mack.

The second reason for this McGwire card's popularity has everything to do with his game. After slugging 49 home runs in his rookie season with the Oakland Athletics, McGwire gained a strong measure of fame and became an instant star. Teamed with José Canseco, another hobby darling, McGwire served notice that he would be around for many years as one of baseball's elite power hitters.

Though his hitting would at times be inconsistent (his batting average sometimes put him dangerously close to the Mendoza Line), there was no denying his power, and in 1998, when baseball was recovering from a strike, McGwire, along with fellow power hitter Sammy Sosa, carried the game on his shoulders as he pursued, and eventually surpassed the game's most illustrious record, which had been held by Roger Maris since 1961.

McGwire's performance during the eclipse year, along with those after it, however, has become mired in controversy: it was revealed he taking Androstenedione, a hormone that increases muscle mass exponentially. Take one look at McGwire on this card and compare him to what he looked like when he broke the record and it's almost like looking at two different people.

The Andro supplements all but launched baseball's darkest time — the so-called Steroid Era. McGwire, Sosa, Rafael Palmeiro, Jason Giambi, Roger Clemens and future home run king Barry Bonds were among the many superstars who were either guilty or at least accused of taking performance enhancers. Suspensions would result and reputations would be tarnished.

The ultimate consequence for McGwire, at least thus far, is that he has not been voted into the Baseball Hall of Fame, and there are few who would argue that McGwire never should be allowed into Cooperstown, nor should any other suspect player from this era. In January 2010, in an attempt to clear the air after refusing to do so in front of a congressional hearing on steroids, he admitted to taking steroids throughout his career.

McGwire's cards took the same hit as his reputation. The demand for the '85 Topps RC is nowhere near what it once was, though some collectors still pick it up, preferring to remember him in the days before controversy killed his marketability. ◄ ◄

WANT TO UNDERSTAND THE concept of triumph under pressure? Consider Roger Maris. Maris wasn't unlike many baseball players of his generation. Born in Hibbing, Minnesota (with a population of just over 17,000 in 2000 according to Wikipedia) as Roger Maras (he changed his last name in 1955), he was the son of Croatian immigrants. His family also lived in Grand Forks and Fargo, North Dakota, where the youngster exceled at football, eventually catching the eyes of scouts at the University of Oklahoma. He didn't take the field, however, and returned to Fargo.

Had he played for the Sooners, who knows what would have become of Major League Baseball's most hallowed record — the most home runs in a single season. In fact, according to the Roger Maris Museum's website, the legend was quoted as once saying, "Baseball was just something to do in the summer."

But it was the long ball that was Maris's true calling, and in 1957 he reached the big leagues, starting his career in Cleveland after signing with the club four years earlier. He spent one year with the Indians before going to the Kansas City Athletics for the 1958 season (the same year he earned his first card), then moved on to the team that would make him a baseball legend — the New York Yankees — in 1960.

By this time, Maris was starting to build his name in the bigs, having played in the 1959 All-Star Game. 1960, however, was his breakout year. He garnered MVP honors after slugging 39 home runs, 112 RBIs and had a career-high .283 batting average.

Yet 1961 would be his crescendo. Throughout much of the year, Maris and teammate Mickey Mantle would battle in a contest of one-upsmanship, with more media-ites and fans backing the Mick. Once Mantle was out of the race, however, Maris was set for a date with destiny.

With or without Mantle by his side, Maris was under stress throughout the entire chase. As the story goes, Maris's hair was falling out in clumps from the pressure he felt. Added to the immeasurable heaviness placed on Maris's shoulders was a ruling by then-commissioner Ford Frick that Maris had to break the record in 154 games, eight shorter than the length of the baseball schedule, as that was the number of contests that made up an MLB season during Babe Ruth's record-setting era.

Maris would not make that date and would instead hit home run number 61 in the final game of the 1961 season. He would win his second MVP award among other accolades, but individuals at the time would asterisk the home run mark.

Before and after the 1962 season, Maris appeared on numerous cards, issued by trading card companies around the world. Even the Roger Maris Museum, situated in Fargo, produced a card at one point.

But of all the hundreds of Maris cards produced (a count at the end of 2009 registered 1,678 according to Beckett.com), none has carried the mystique of capturing the home run chase like the 1962 Topps issue.

The card is number one in that year's release, a subtle honor that was as much a poison as it was a pleasure. Finding a '62 Maris in good condition is a difficult thing to accomplish — almost as difficult as hitting 61 home runs in one season, regardless of how many games one plays. ◀◀◀

1994 SP
ALEX RODRIGUEZ

THE STEROID ERA HAS claimed the legacy of many of the most popular superstars of the '90s and early 2000s, with many high profile players' reputations being irreparably tarnished.

Perhaps the only one to have survived relatively unscathed is Alex Rodriguez. The one-time understudy to Ken Griffey Jr. had been on the fast track to immortality when, prior to the 2009 season, word broke that A-Rod had allegedly taken steroids between 2001 and 2003 while he was still with Seattle. The poster child for the New York Yankees had, all of a sudden, become the latest in a series of superstars to be branded with baseball's equivalent of the scarlet letter.

But something odd happened: rather than being shunned by fans, A-Rod continued doing what he does best — being a subject of fan adoration and Hollywood gossip.

Like other New York athletes, Rodriguez was one of the few baseball players who truly transcended his sport and was a hot name wherever he went. In the tradition of Joe DiMaggio, Rodriguez at one point dated a blond Hollywood starlet (Kate Hudson, not Madonna as was rumored), and just like Joe Namath, A-Rod got involved in commercial endorsements, like for the *Guitar Hero: Aerosmith* video game.

Through it all, Rodriguez maintained a strong standing in the hobby. Though he appeared on the market after the boom had begun to fizzle, A-Rod's were still some of the most antici-pated rookie cards to be busted from packs.

The most important of these was this card, from Upper Deck's SP series. Now as older fans will remember, SP was one of those post-boom sets that came out with unmistakable allure — it felt expensive, it looked expensive, and with pack prices that crossed the then unheard of five dollar plateau, it *was* expensive.

Of course, the name itself oozed limited edition. Though Upper Deck never told collectors what SP stood for (and hasn't to this day, despite offshoot brands like SPx and SP Authentic being thrown into the mix), the two letters were already very familiar to hobbyists, meaning single print or special print.

As a result, the hype machine was fully functional when SP, like other UD products, was first test run with baseball; indeed, it was an unbridled success. Collectors clamored for the A-Rod and many other cards in the series.

Of course, the collector base had shrunk a fair bit by this time — the investment crew had already left the hobby — so there was plenty to go around for collectors who were willing to plunk down the extra cash. But no one seemed to mind. After all, collectors had been swamped by all-too familiar brands for so many years that a different set by UD, its first major product release that wasn't the base brand name, was bound to be a hit.

Since that release, A-Rod has proved to be a very hot com-modity, and even though he and Upper Deck haven't always been on the best of terms (during his tenure as Topps spokes-person, UD mocked A-Rod, by packing out cards featuring him in a few different jerseys as he wavered about whether he'd continue with the Yanks or not), this card has remained one of the most popular UD ever produced. ◀ ◀ ◀

O.J. SIMPSON

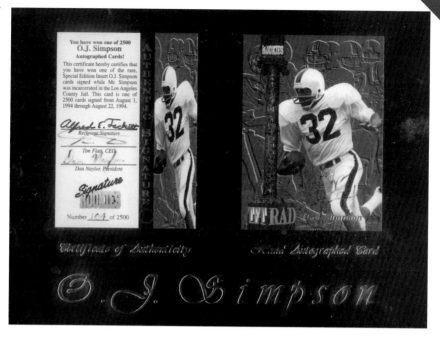

IN THE MID-1990s, A SMALL COMPANY CALLED SIGNATURE ROOKIES produced limited cards featuring young prospects along with a handful of sporting legends. The cards weren't licensed, but they did have some appeal to collectors who wanted to pull a certified autograph in each pack.

The format worked and they enjoyed short-term success. But there was a pivotal moment, outside of the company's control, that brought it from relative obscurity to national media attention — the arrest of former football star O.J. Simpson. A standout at the collegiate level and with the NFL's Buffalo Bills, he was a superstar in the 1970s and had remained in the spotlight in retirement as an actor and spokesman. In 1994, he was in the spotlight for a different reason, accused of the murder of his ex-wife, Nicole Brown Simpson, and her companion, Ron Goldman.

The media circus surrounding Simpson's run from the law, arrest and trial was incredible, and journalists also managed to pick up on the fact that he was obligated to sign some cards for Signature Rookies for its upcoming Tetrad release. In fact, he had signed a contract with the company four days before the murders. While the company did question whether it was legal to uphold the contract, it went ahead with the deal and earned a permanent place in hobby history.

People magazine reported that Simpson was allegedly being paid $100,000 to sign 2,500 cards while in prison and the hobby's reaction was a mix of intrigue and disgust. Many dealers refused to carry the product while others looked at the release as an opportunity to make a quick buck. This situation was made even crazier by the fact that Signature Rookies would create additional cards of Simpson for other products. Some collectors certainly shied away from Signature Rookies for a variety of reasons (shoddy designs, less-than-limited print runs and rumors that autographed cards had been forged, to name a few) and the company eventually descended into oblivion.

The legacy of Signature Rookies essentially boils down to a single trading card, and it was one for the ages. While Simpson was eventually found criminally not guilty, he was found guilty in a civil trial and ordered to pay restitution, while he vowed to "search for the real killers." Persona-non-grata in the trading card and sports memorabilia industry, he did make an unauthorized appearance at the 2005 National Sports Collectors Convention in Chicago — and was escorted out of the building Later that day, collectors could find him selling his signature for cash at a neighboring hotel.

Two years later, Simpson, along with a group of men, held a sports memorabilia dealer at gun point. On December 5, 2008, he was sentenced to 33 years in prison. ◀ ◀ ◀

1984 DONRUSS
DON MATTINGLY

IN THE EARLY '80s, THE NEW York Yankees were in an odd position — they weren't a superstar-laden team. Once you got past Dave Winfield, the roster thinned pretty quickly. Willie Randolph, Dave Righetti and Ken Griffey Sr. were stars in their own right, but there wasn't the Broadway-level player to match Winfield for big name glory. It was a far different era than the heady days when tandems like Babe Ruth and Lou Gehrig, Mickey Mantle and Roger Maris or Reggie Jackson and Catfish Hunter were the big kids on the block. One guy shouldered all of the hope and expectations of Yanks fans, and it wasn't until 1984 that another well-hyped superstar would emerge — Don Mattingly.

Mattingly first arrived in the big leagues in 1982. He impressed during his first year, but was unable to earn a starting job with the Yankees — first base was held by Steve Balboni, who patrolled for the pinstripers through 1983. It wasn't until '84, in fact, that Mattingly was given his chance to shine — and so he did. He beat Winfield to lead the majors in batting average (.343), claiming the crown in the final game of the season. That year, he was also the league leader in doubles and was second in slugging percentage.

One year later, Mattingly cemented his legacy: he won the American League's MVP award, was first in doubles and runs batted in, and collected his first Golden Glove award. He'd add eight more by the time his career was finished.

As Mattingly's reputation grew, so too did his collector base. He would start to appear on packaging for cards and his name would frequently be mentioned in early collecting circles. Even at that early stage, there were more products that bore Donnie Baseball's image than one could imagine. Topps led the way in many respects, creating everything from mini cards to buttons to rub-on tattoos. Donruss, for its part, wasn't to be outdone, featuring him in its Diamond Kings subset and creating a special card of Mattingly and Winfield in 1985. Fleer produced a special edition series and stickers that highlighted, you guessed it, Mattingly among its roster of stars.

But it was the 1984 Donruss RC that reigned over all of his other cards. Most other rookie cards of the era would come from the Traded or Update box series (hence, for a while, earning the XRC designation from leading sports card price guide *Beckett*), giving Donruss, still a young buck at the time, the opportunity to issue one of its greatest cards, if not its single greatest card, of the 1980s.

Even though Donnie Baseball never won the World Series as a player, and the market has seen continued releases of Mattingly cards since the '80s, including hundreds of pieces since his retirement, it's the Donruss rookie that stands above all others of the most recognized and loved Yankee of his era. ◀ ◀ ◀

EMMITT SMITH   COWBOYS™

IN 1989, SCORE WAS THE toast of the football trading card world after releasing a short run and popular debut set. Hobbyists everywhere wondered if lightning would strike twice when its 1990 product hit the market. There were high hopes, but the Texas-based company let the presses run and created a monster that may have been one of the biggest bombs the industry has ever seen.

After the debacle of their regular set, they decided to put out a Supplemental collection and wisely scaled back production. However, they might have scaled back a little too much: many who had put the basic set together scrambled to get the Supplemental cards in their hands, and prices began to rise due to the presence of Dallas Cowboys super rookie Emmitt Smith.

In his first season, Smith was part of a rebuilding Cowboys club; he would rush for 937 yards on his way to being named the NFL's Offensive Rookie of the Year. As a result, all of his cards were hot commodities and he had rookie cards in four different update sets (Score, Fleer, Action Packed and Topps) and the second series from Pro Set. Over the next few years, he would become one of the game's greatest, reeling off 11 straight seasons with 1,000 or more yards in addition to winning the Super Bowl on three occasions.

Throughout his career, Smith battled for hobby supremacy

with Barry Sanders of the Detroit Lions, and both are considered at the same level of collectability. While Sanders retired prematurely with several strong seasons potentially still ahead of him, Smith stuck around and managed to become the NFL's all-time leader in rushing. He broke that record during his last season with Dallas in 2002, and he would play two more seasons with the Arizona Cardinals before hanging up his cleats for good.

Oddly, Smith's post-football career would be filled with CV highlights that one wouldn't expect to encourage collectors to come back for more. One such venture was his appearance on the ABC series *Dancing with the Stars*. Not only did he compete on the show, but he was part of the winning pair. He also began endorsing Just for Men, a line of hair coloring gels — not something you'd think would inspire Generation X and Y to want to go out and grab his collectibles. Still, hobbyists scour message boards for both older and recent issues featuring the running back.

As time passes, the Score Supplemental set should still continue to be the Smith rookie card of choice, especially since his career rushing record looks like it might not be broken for a long time. As the youth of the 1990s age, they may also become nostalgic for the football stars of their era — which means demand should remain high as people return to collecting cards. By today's standards, there are more than enough copies of this card to go around, but there is a certain perception of its scarcity that ensures that it remains popular. ◀◀

ODE TO THE '90s

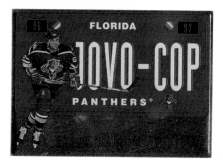

▶ METAL CARDS

In the endless effort to offer collectors something different, card companies, primarily Leaf/Donruss and a couple minor sellers, offered up cards on pieces of metal for a few years in the '90s. Ranging from tin to 24-karat gold, these cards are among the most kitschy of all pieces ever issued.

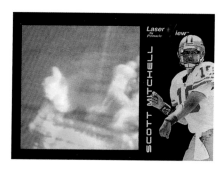

▶ POGS

Milkcaps were a popular toy for baby boomers to play with as kids, but for collectors in the '90s, they were *the* hot collectible for a brief period. Several sets were released, including by the signature POG company, but it was Classic Games Inc. that upped the cheese factor with releases like this Shaq disc.

▶ MOTION CARDS

Why settle for a picture when you can get a miniature video? Card companies experimented with motion cards that captured game action on cardboard with lenticular or hologram technology, producing some very unique pieces. Sportflics had experimented with multi-image cards in the '80s, but weren't able to make smooth motion capture cards like these '90s releases.

▶ "TWO-SPORT" ATHLETES

Though Bo Jackson and Deion Sanders legitimately played in two professional leagues at once, card companies devoted space in some 1990s sets to athletes in sport shots outside their own. Score was first out of the gate, issuing a card of Eric Lindros in its baseball set after the prospect took to batting practice with the Toronto Blue Jays.

▶ DIE CUTS

The thought of not having a perfectly rectangular card probably would've made '80s collectors faint, but '90s collectors embraced die-cut cards. Some of the shapes and designs were actually quite remarkable, though some extremes meant that cards were more condition sensitive than ever. The die-cutting trend continues to have a strong presence today.

▶ FOILBOARD

Regular cardboard has its limits. Put as much metallic ink as you want on a card to make it shimmer, but it's still not going to shine. Enter foilboard and the technology that allowed images to be printed on the metallic surface. Every company has used foilboard at one point or another, to the delight (or dismay) of collectors, since it debuted in the '90s. ◀◀◀

PETE
MARAVICH
forward
ATLANTA

THERE ARE FEW ATHLETES who compare to the man known as "Pistol Pete."

Pete Maravich is one of basketball's tragic heroes. A standout from his days at Louisiana State University, Maravich was destined for NBA greatness, and his brief career proved that the expectations heaped upon him were well placed.

Known affectionately as "Pistol" since high school, Maravich entered the NBA with the Atlanta Hawks after being the third overall selection in the 1970 draft. He made headlines instantly when the Hawks signed him to a $1.9 million contract, making him one of the richest players in the NBA at that time. No one can say that he didn't earn the big dollars though, as he made the All-Rookie Team after averaging 23.2 points per game.

Even at the time, one can imagine Maravich's RC being in high demand. After all, here was a guy who was stellar on the court and had the back-home charm that would've had girls swooning and guys jealous (okay, on second thought, maybe he wouldn't have been highly collected).

At this point, Topps was still committed to creating basketball cards and was seemingly going to stay in the hobby. And it would, for many years, but even with the draw of Larry Bird and Magic Johnson, Topps would leave basketball, letting Fleer and Star take over the market.

Topps would eventually return to this segment of the hobby in the early 1990s, as would the format for the Maravich rookie — the Tall Boy. For some reason, the extend-o-cards that were high in kitsch factor in the 1960s were issued more than once in basketball, which is mystifying yet in a way appropriate. (Makes you wonder why there weren't Wide Boys for the buffet busters of football.) If you can imagine how many standard-size cards fell victim to soft edges before, just imagine how much damage was incurred on these bad boys.

Maravich's rookie is also another rare example from the vintage era of a first-year player's card debuting at the same time as he started playing. Judging by the photo, which has Maravich holding a basketball over the spot where a team crest would be, Topps apparently chose to take this photo early on and then built the rest of the design around it.

Maravich would go on to have a very solid career, as a five-time NBA All-Star who twice made both the first and second All-NBA teams. His tenure, however, was cut short due to a leg injury in the 1977–78 season, and by 1980 he had withdrawn from the league. Maravich went on to lead a quiet life, largely away from the sport. His story would end unfortunately early; he died in 1988, at just 40 years of age, less than a year after being inducted into basketball's Hall of Fame.

Since his passing, Maravich's legacy has thrived. His auctioned memorabilia continues to be in high demand, as does this card. ◀◀◀

SINCE THE BEGINNING OF THE boom era, collectors in all sports have been clamoring for autograph cards that feature the best in the game from the past and present. But once in a while, a card appears that sets the collecting world on fire. For hockey enthusiasts, that occurred during the 2000–01 season when Upper Deck finally brought Gordie Howe, Bobby Orr and Wayne Gretzky together on cardboard for the first time.

The idea of having an autograph from any one of these players is appealing, but the idea of combining them together on the same card blew everyone away. The 2000–01 SP Authentic product was limited to just 25 copies — it's one of those rare hobby treasures that rocks the collectibles landscape.

Interestingly, all three players skated during the same season in 1978–79. Howe was winding down his career with the New England Whalers and Gretzky split his first pro campaign between the Indianapolis Racers and the Edmonton Oilers of the World Hockey Association. At the same time, Orr was playing his last pro games with the Chicago Blackhawks, before knee woes prematurely ended his pro career.

As a child, Gretzky idolized Howe and the two would play together for the WHA All-Stars in 1979, but there was only one game of note that really connected Orr and Gretzky. On April 25, 1980, a benefit game was held in Winnipeg, Manitoba, for injured player Bill Heindl and the two players skated together for the only time.

Surprisingly, Upper Deck has been conservative in issuing the tri-auto in different series. Despite having all three legends under contract for many years, the combination of hockey's holy trinity has rarely been repeated. That being said, it makes sense to limit a card of this magnitude to avoid overexposure.

It is hard to say if this card will appreciate in value since there is always the chance that the company could release the same combination in a new product. As of January 2010, the triple autograph has a book value of $2,500, but there are few sales to track just 10 years after the product was released. It is safe to say that many are firmly lodged in personal collections and when they do surface for sale, they are quickly scooped up. Strangely, a similar card that came two years later has a book value of $1,500. That difference of $1,000 is puzzling since it is the exact same combination of players and also numbered to 25. One suggestion for budget-conscious collectors is to instead obtain individual certified autographs of the three players, which is a goal that can be accomplished for $500 or less. ◀ ◀

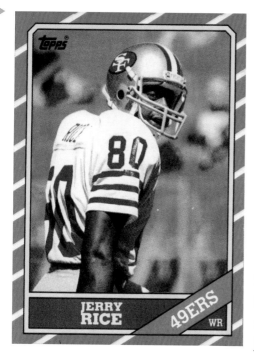

CARD COLLECTORS INVARIABLY flock to greatness, and for close to 20 years the 1986 Jerry Rice Topps rookie card has been a popular, consistent seller both in hobby stores and online.

The San Francisco 49ers made Rice the 16th overall pick in the 1985 NFL Draft, and he would have a strong pro start with 927 receiving yards. His career really started to take off in his sophomore season: he led the league with 1,570 receiving yards and scored 15 touchdowns. That year, he was voted to the first of what would become 13 Pro Bowl appearances, and savvy collectors started to set aside his first trading card.

The 1986 Topps Football set is notoriously tough to find in top condition due to its colored borders. They resemble a football field and can chip if you breathe on them the wrong way. The design is still one of the best of the 1980s and the 396-card set was loaded with a good mix of hot rookies like Rice, Reggie White, Boomer Esiason, as well as Rice's future teammate Steve Young (who had a card in the Topps USFL set two years earlier that's been assigned an XRC tag since it was only available in boxed set form) and the biggest stars of the day. Over time, the set has been praised by collectors, and many enthusiasts appreciate the challenge of putting together a high-grade set.

Over 21 NFL seasons spent with San Francisco, Oakland

and Seattle, Rice would become the sport's all-time leader in receiving yards (22,895) and achieve a number of other standards for wide receivers. A three-time Super Bowl champ, he's also the league's all-time leader in touchdowns (with 197 regular season touchdown and 207 in total). With Steve Young, Rice formed one of the all-time greatest quarterback-receiver combinations in NFL history, as the two would account for the vast majority of those TDs and would be a constant threat to put points up on the board, whether they were in the red zone or on their own side of the 50-yard line. While some may argue that his totals are impressive because of his longevity, he was still a dominant force for most of his career.

As an investment, the Rice rookie card is a recommended pickup — especially if it can be acquired in top condition. A collector who takes a chance on buying some rack packs or a vending box from the 1986 season could potentially pull a copy of this card that could be professionally graded and sold for a tidy profit. A gem mint copy of the card that was graded a 10 by PSA was sold by Heritage Auctions in 2009 for $2,509, and it really is a treasure to behold. There is likely to be consistent demand for this card, and since Rice was inducted into the Pro Football Hall of Fame in 2010, there may also be a temporary surge in its popularity. ◀ ◀

MARTIN BRODEUR   G
New Jersey Devils

WHAT WERE THEY THINKING?

In 1990–91, Upper Deck and Pro Set were both on the rookie bandwagon, creating cards of virtually any player who laced up a pair of skates prior to or during the regular season, no matter how slim their chances were of making the National Hockey League their permanent place of business.

Both companies had draft picks (albeit UD's pool was a bit deeper), so there was no excuse for excluding a player who would go on to become arguably the greatest goaltender of all time. But that's what happened to Martin Brodeur.

Sure, he was a goofy-faced kid with a bad teenage mustache on draft day, but is that any reason to keep him from your card set? And yes, there wasn't really a huge collector base for New Jersey Devils cards, but does that mean that their draft picks shouldn't make it into a set?

We could offer other excuses, but really, there's no reason Brodeur wasn't on any company's checklist after the NHL's 1990 Entry Draft. If for no other reason than his lineage (his father, Denis, was a goalie for Canada's national team and a leading photographer for the Montreal Canadiens), Brodeur should have been included.

Instead, only Score recognized his potential and put him in its draft set. Although, it's worth noting that Score, like all the other companies, did miss out on future 500 goal scorer Keith

Tkachuk because he was still playing for Boston University.

So why did Score succeed where UD and Pro Set failed? The answer may be found on the back of Brodeur's, and other players', cards. In a usual practice — but one that clearly isn't being followed as often as it should be — Score included quotes from NHL scouts and team personnel in its card-back write-ups. That kind of research inevitably results in a larger representation of players who might otherwise have been looked over.

Of course, it also helped that Score had 440 cards, the largest opening series of any company that included prospects from North America — Pro Set's first series was 405 cards; Upper Deck had 400. (Topps and O-Pee-Chee, while larger, did not include draft picks or AHLers.) The larger checklist meant that Score had the opportunity to include additional prospects like Kölzig and Kris Draper in its first set, beating other companies by a few months.

But the real diamond in the rough was Brodeur. He would go on to become one of hockey's top stars, and in the eyes of many fans, the best goalie of all time. Brodeur would establish new standards for wins, including most seasons with 40 wins and most wins in a season. But the most important record he holds is the one that most NHL pundits thought would never be broken — the longstanding 103 shutout record held by Terry Sawchuk.

Brodeur would also capture several Vézina trophies, anchor three Stanley Cup–winning teams and win gold with Team Canada at the 2002 and 2010 Winter Olympics and the 2004 World Cup of Hockey.

Some goalies are better than Brodeur in specific areas of the game, but no one had as complete and impressive an overall record as the man who, in a time when everyone was being scooped up by every card company, can only claim one RC. Though neither the Canadian or American version are in short supply (the two are differentiated by the color of Score's logo on the card's face), finding one of these cards today in a pack is like striking gold. ◄ ◄

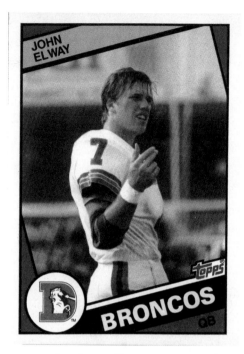

WHEN THE FOOTBALL CARD market began to pick up steam in the early 1990s, there were a number of quarterbacks collectors wanted most, and while John Elway may not have had the widespread popularity of Joe Montana and Dan Marino, he was no slouch, having lead the Denver Broncos to three Super Bowl appearances in the 1980s and managing to put up superstar-level offense as well.

Elway's only rookie card was part of the 1984 Topps Football effort. He was a lock to be considered a part of that set since he was the first overall pick in the 1983 NFL draft out of Stanford University by the Baltimore Colts. He refused to suit up for the club and they traded him to the Broncos on May 2 of that year. Also a prospect in the New York Yankees organization at the time, he ultimately chose to pursue a football career, and his first season saw him pass for 1,663 yards and score seven touchdowns. Denver finished the season with a 9–7 record to place second in the AFC West.

The Elway rookie card began to gather more steam as the 1990s progressed and he proved himself one of the most consistent quarterbacks in NFL history. His numbers were always among the league's leaders, and in 1993 he had a monster season that saw him being named the league's Offensive Player of the Year by UPI. This card was always sought after by collectors throughout his career, but it moved up as one of the hobby's hottest as the end of the decade neared and he showed the football world that he could win the big game.

In 1997, he helped the Broncos to a 12–4 record and rolled over the Jacksonville Jaguars in a wild card game before defeating the Kansas City Chiefs and Pittsburgh Steelers for the right to go to the Super Bowl. Denver defeated the Green Bay Packers with a score of 31–24, and Elway rushed for a single touchdown during the contest. The club didn't rest on its laurels though, as it went to the Super Bowl once again the following season; the QB was named the game's Most Valuable Player after passing for 336 yards and scoring twice in a 34–19 victory over the Atlanta Falcons. It was the last time Elway would step out onto the gridiron, and he would enter the Pro Football Hall of Fame in 2004.

It's hard to say if there will be a long-term demand for Elway's rookie card, but it is certainly an important one to have if you are a football card collector. While it has often been overshadowed by the Marino card from the same set, it has become a piece that's often viewed at the same level by many collectors. As with the Marino, there are counterfeit copies out there, and it suffers from the same production issues common in Topps products from the era. ◀ ◀

SOMETIMES YOU HAVE TO wonder if card companies ever properly research their subjects. After all, why else would cards continue to appear with the wrong name attributed to a player, or a player named as part of the wrong team?

Some of these snafus are downright funny. Cal Ripken Jr., arguably one of the top 10 most recognized athletes of the 1980s, has had his name misspelled a couple times. Pro Set actually developed a cult following of collectors trying to gather every one of its error cards.

But perhaps the biggest slip-up in the history of sports cards came from Topps, using the trademark Gum Inc., which went far beyond any mere typo.

The error occurred in the 1956 Adventure set. The concept for the product was one that has grown in popularity as the "big four" sports have become increasingly multinational — cards that featured an athlete's country of origin. Since that set was issued, almost every company, including Parkhurst, Topps and Upper Deck have integrated players' nationalities in one form or another.

Though athleticism is supposedly apolitical, sometimes world politics creep into sports and into sports cards too. And that was the case with this set, which featured 20 boxers, including Max Schmeling.

Boxing historians will no doubt count Schmeling as one of

the greatest pugilists in the sport's history. The German fighter became the world champion in 1930 after defeating Jack Sharkey by disqualification (making Schmeling still the only title holder to claim his belt after such a victory) and later he was the first to upend the famous Joe Louis, beating him in 1936.

All of this took place during the rise of Nazi party in Germany, and Schmeling soon became the poster boy for the new German rulers. In his 1938 rematch against Louis, Schmeling was portrayed as an Aryan villain in contrast to the American hero. Schmeling, however, was no Nazi. Not only did he employ an American Jewish trainer, he famously hid two teenage boys during the Kristallnacht atrocity that took place the year of the rematch with Louis.

In their second contest, Schmeling was TKO'd by Louis, though the bout carried a measure of controversy: there were accusations post-fight of illegal shots to Schmeling's kidneys.

Schmeling, for his part, was more than happy that the decision stood. "Looking back, I'm almost happy I lost that fight. Just imagine if I would have come back to Germany with a victory. I had nothing to do with the Nazis, but they would have given me a medal. After the war I might have been considered a war criminal," Schmeling said in a 1975 interview that was recorded on Auschwitz.dk, a Holocaust memorial website.

As you can imagine, this card, which features Schmeling with a swastika in the background, wasn't well received. Distributed in vending machines, the card was very quickly pulled from circulation. Few samples in good condition exist today. ◀ ◀

1989-90 HOOPS
DAVID ROBINSON

DAVID ROBINSON

SPURS   CENTER

IN 1989, BOTH THE TRADING card market and the world of sports were very different places, but there was a movement beginning that would see both generate unbelievable revenues from a public that wanted more options for its collecting dollars. That year saw the debut of Upper Deck in baseball, the arrival of Pro Set and Score in football and the arrival of Hoops for basketball fans.

At first glance, Hoops appeared a welcome addition to the hobby, since basketball collectors had often had only a single option available. For the previous three seasons, Fleer had the market to itself and had produced some great cards. But with Hoops, you were getting a clean design along with great action photography and a massive 300-card set that was endorsed by the NBA itself. Where Hoops had a major advantage over its competition was with the inclusion of rookie David Robinson of the San Antonio Spurs, who was shown on his card holding up his jersey at a press conference instead of in game action.

Sales of the inaugural Hoops set were more than brisk, and the company decided to see if lightning would strike twice when it released a second series later in the season. In a strange move, they decided to keep the set at 300 cards and substituted traded and retired players with rookies. As a result, those who were late to the game and started collecting with the update could not complete their set. While such a move by a manufacturer would not be tolerated in today's market, it proved to be a boon for those who had the first series boxes, sets and singles.

The first Robinson card (#138) was replaced by one with an action shot (#310), creating a massive demand for the initial card. Collectors demanded the first one by a greater margin, and the price kept rising as Robinson emerged as one of the sport's top stars. Hoops also produced a yellow-bordered set of cards to be sold at Sears stores, but they are not as highly sought-after as the actual rookie card.

Robinson went on to play 14 seasons in the NBA and was the league's Rookie of the Year in 1989–90. Five years later, he earned Most Valuable Player honors and went on to lead the Spurs to a pair of championships as well. Now a member of the Basketball Hall of Fame, he is considered to be one of the top stars of the 1990s, often commended for both his offensive and defensive abilities.

The demand for this Robinson rookie card eventually subsided, but it basically launched a company that helped change the way the hobby treated basketball. ◀ ◀

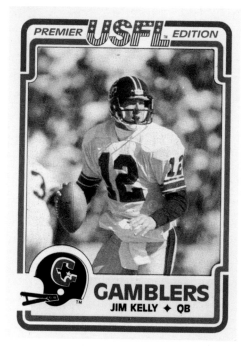

IT'S HARD TO IMAGINE THAT an athlete who lost four consecutive championship games would even come close to making a list like this, but Jim Kelly, star quarterback for the Buffalo Bills, wasn't an ordinary four-time loser.

The Bills, as you may know, are the epitome of a football team that, to borrow from basketball, can't buy a bucket. Sure, they reached the Super Bowl every year from 1991 to 1994, an incredible streak no matter how you slice it, but they also gained a reputation as big-game chokers. Whether it was a botched field goal attempt or folding like a cheap umbrella, the Bills couldn't get it done in the only contest that really counted in an NFL season.

So why in the name of Vince Lombardi are we talking about Jim Kelly? Because, despite his lack of playoff success, he really was that damn good.

In his illustrious career, Kelly only threw less than 2,800 yards once, and that was in a season he played just 12 games. Only twice (one time being his rookie season) did he have a sub-.500 record, and in six of his seasons he won at least 10 games. Kelly was voted into the NFL Hall of Fame in 2002 and is widely considered one of the best QBs both of his generation and in the history of the gridiron.

As if this wasn't enough, Kelly's rookie card came out at a very — how shall we say? — opportune time. Like basketball and hockey, football had a challenger to the throne as *the* elite football organization.

Only it wasn't.

Sure, the United States Football League lasted longer than other also-rans (read: Xtreme Football League) and produced more eventual NFL superstars, but it was doomed from the start — even before it dared challenge the NFL by attempting to move to a fall schedule.

Not long after the league began, the bubble burst, and like the World Hockey Association/National Hockey League and American Basketball Association/National Basketball Association that preceded them, the NFL and USFL would ultimately become one league. (Funny how that word "national" reigned supreme in each of those sports, yet America's "national pastime" doesn't have that word in its highest-ranking pro league. We're just saying.)

The USFL, however, does live on in cards. Topps, not being one to ever let an opportunity pass (yes, they even created an XFL series), took a chance and released USFL sets, highlighted by cards like Kelly's. Several other football stars were also part of the release, but no card has kept its mystique like the one pictured here. ◄ ◄

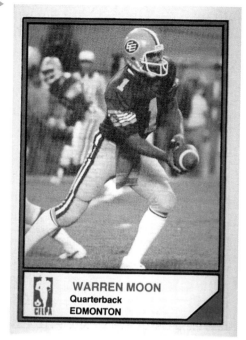

WARREN MOON
Quarterback
EDMONTON

THIS ONE MAY TAKE SOME explanation for American readers, so bear with us.

It's not because Americans aren't aware of the Canadian Football League — in fact, most Yanks have likely heard of the football league that, for most of its existence, has been isolated above the 49th parallel (a few years of experimentation brought three-down football to U.S. markets such as Baltimore, Birmingham and Las Vegas). The success of some of the CFL's top exports to the NFL can't be denied. Of late, these have included Doug Flutie and Mike Vanderjagt — but perhaps the greatest player to go south after plying his trade in the CFL was Warren Moon.

Moon was one of the most dominant three-down quarterbacks ever. Despite only playing six seasons with the Edmonton Eskimos, he led the club to five consecutive Grey Cups and amassed an incredible 21,000-plus yards, including 5,648 in his final season (1983), a CFL record. For this, Moon was honored as the CFL's Most Outstanding Player; his other honors included being twice named the Grey Cup MVP and being named to the CFL Hall of Fame in 2001.

His tenure in the NFL, primarily with the Houston Oilers, was equally dominant. He set an Oilers franchise record for passing with 3,338 yards in his first season with the club, and later exceeded the 4,000-yard plateau twice with Houston and two more times with Minnesota. In 1990, he was named the NFL offensive MVP, and seven years later as the 1997 Pro Bowl MVP he proved he was still at the top of his game. Moon would be inducted into the NFL Hall of Fame in 2006.

With all of these accolades, how is it that a CFL card stands above all of his others? For that, you need to know the history of CFL's collector series. Several companies have held licenses over the years, including Topps, O-Pee-Chee, Pacific and Extreme, as well as small-run companies like REL and All-World.

But the company that has had the longest tenure with the CFL is JOGO, which curiously maintained a very simple production agenda. Only a couple times in the company's history did it release anything other than a boxed set (in the early 1990s, packs with inserts and parallels were part of its distribution) and the quantities have always been painfully limited. As the story goes, there were an equal number of sets given to the players as there were produced for fans.

While most NFL series would count thousands of base sets (once assembled), most JOGO sets only numbered into the hundreds, and considering the die-hard following that the series held, singles very rarely appear on the open market.

The 1983 Moon card is an interesting card in itself — it has very high demand among CFL collectors despite the fact that it is not his rookie card. The first Moon card came out in 1981 as part of JOGO's debut CFL release, but that set was an oversized issue and collectors don't hold it in the same regard as the standard-sized 1983 edition.

Also, unlike most sets produced during that time, the photography is black and white, as are the graphical touches of the team helmets, on the '83 card.

Regardless of the card's aesthetic appeal, the Warren Moon rookie card remains one of, if not the most, desirable of all CFL trading cards. ◀ ◀

1990 SCORE "BO"
BO JACKSON

IT'S A PRETTY innocuous card at first glance — two-sport athlete Bo Jackson wearing football shoulder pads, with a baseball bat balanced across his shoulders. It's such a great picture you almost wish it was a poster.

Guess what? It was. And that's why it's such a controversial card.

No one's quite sure what Score was thinking when it produced this. Then again, we can make a pretty accurate guess, given that Jackson was 1990's hottest athlete — period. His football and baseball rookie cards were in high demand and companies did all they could in the pre–auto and jersey era to generate more buzz.

With Bo, Score was the company that was most on the ball, pardon the pun. It seemed like they produced more Jackson cards in that short span than anyone. And we do mean short — Jackson's two-sport career was all but over after injuring his hip in a January 1991 NFL playoff game. Football quickly became a distant memory, but Jackson soldiered on in baseball for a few more seasons despite losing a lot of his superhuman speed.

But back to the "BO" card. Score created this unique offering as a kind of predecessor to the Dream Team subset cards it would issue a year later, which also featured artistic black-and-white photography (including, bizarrely, that shirtless José Canseco card we'd all like to forget). Confused? So were collectors of the era, who were even more mystified when a company called Ultimate issued similar black-and-white photo cards of 1991 NHL Entry Draft players — some of whom were only bedecked in towels.

But it was the "BO" that stuck out in the new black-and-white trend, and for the wrong reasons. Mysteriously, it features a photo that was also used in a Nike poster. A quick change of the logo and you have one image on two different collectibles.

The word was that Score hadn't secured the proper permission to use the photo. Of course, controversy creates cash, and even if the buzz was the stuff of urban legend, the growing baseball card market ate up the news like it was a ballpark frank, grossly inflating the price of otherwise dollar bin fodder to unheard-of listings of $20 or more.

Score sensed that it had lightning trapped in a bottle and went for a two-peat of its success the following year, creating the 1991 "Bo Breaker" card. The card, however, didn't have nearly the same impact as the "BO." Perhaps this is because the card got lost in the shuffle of a mammoth set totaling 893 cards (and no, that doesn't include inserts). Collectors were overwhelmed by the size of the series; it was the cardboard equivalent of jumping the shark.

Score was never able to recover from the 1991 debacle. A few years later it changed its name to Pinnacle Brands Inc. Today, the Score name can still be found as part of Panini's lineup, while Bo Jackson cards pop up in baseball sets from time to time — without pictures also used by Nike. ◄ ◄

WHEN JACKIE ROBINSON BROKE BASEBALL'S color barrier he did more than simply open the door for African Americans: the man who proudly wore Dodger blue also set the stage for players of other backgrounds to enter the league. Before Jackie, xenophobia dominated America's pastime, but after him, players from across Latin America soon came in as well, including the legendary Roberto Clemente, Juan Marichal and countless others.

The one barrier that remained unbroken for decades involved the Land of the Rising Sun. Though Japanese leagues would occasionally bring in North American imports, Japanese players were reluctant to ply their trade in the States. It wasn't until men like Hideo Nomo and Hideki Matsui made the brave leap to Los Angeles and New York that more of their countrymen began to feel comfortable about heading overseas.

Among those pioneers was Ichiro Suzuki. As with Nomo, Matsui and many others, Suzuki arrived in America to much fanfare. Word had already spread about his amazing work at the plate when he landed in Grunge City, USA. Almost immediately, he made an impact with the Mariners — and just as quickly he became a sensation in the card market. Ichiro's legend would continue to grow as he became one of the most consistent hitters in the game and, in the midst of baseball's most controversial record-breaking era, broke one of its most longstanding records, the most hits in a season, held previously by George Sisler.

Unlike McGwire or Bonds, not an ounce of suspicion surrounded Ichiro. He's become the franchise player in Seattle and the city's most popular athlete since Ken Griffey Jr.'s heyday. Though the Mariners have not been a playoff team since Ichiro joined the squad, his stardom has never been in doubt.

Becoming the second-fastest batter to ever reach the 2,000-hit plateau in 2009 cemented his spot as one of the era's elite in both fans' and collectors' minds.

That's just one of the reasons why this card has maintained its lofty position in the hobby. The other has to do with the SP Authentic set. Unlike so many other brands that have come and gone, SPA, across all the sports it's issued for, has maintained a standing as the must-have set and a destination for anyone who wants to get a highly coveted rookie card. Pick any sport and you're bound to pay a premium for an SPA RC, whether it's autographed or not.

It's been an amazing run for the brand. SP Authentic dates back to the late 1990s, when the SP brand that Upper Deck had used effectively through the early to mid-'90s expanded into new sets, including SPx and SP Game Used. The designs of the cards have largely stayed uniform, over sports and over the years, utilizing a white background.

Though some of his rookies are more valuable (such as the 2001 Upper Deck Ultimate Collection piece), the SP Authentic card gets our nod to represent Ichiro Suzuki, one of the greatest players from Japan to play in baseball's major leagues. ◀ ◀

Note: The card, as pictured, features an in-person autograph.

JOHN L. SULLIVAN.
ALLEN & GINTER'S
RICHMOND. Cigarettes VIRGINIA.

IT'S HARD TO SAY WHICH OF THE MULTI-sport sets created by cigarette companies is the true landmark — the set that all others must be measured against. Certainly, the case could be made for any number of series that have been preserved for well over a century, such as Mayo, Goodwin and, of course, the American Cigarette Company, but there's perhaps more mystique to the Allen & Ginter's World Champions series.

Beginning in 1887 and continuing for a few years, Allen & Ginter produced some of the hobby's simplest-designed yet most spectacular-looking cards. Using a white background, A&Gs (as they are commonly called) have dazzling artistic impressions of athletes from sports such as baseball, wrestling, billiards and boxing. The series includes many stars, but the most famous of all, arguably, is the legendary John L. Sullivan.

Sullivan was boxing's undisputed world champion (yes, there was a time when the title wasn't split between multiple governing bodies) during the time when the sport transitioned from bare knuckles to gloves. In the latter style, he held the world title for an astounding 10 years (though he did not defend between July 8, 1889 and September 7, 1892).

Sullivan's most famous fight may have been his bout against Jake Kilrain on July 8, 1889. Contested under London Prize Ring rules, the bout was the last for the world title without gloves. The match was the first sporting event to have national coverage in the U.S., and it received an unbelievable amount of pre-match attention. Interestingly, the fight was to take place in New Orleans, but it had to be moved when the governor of Louisiana decided it could not be held in his state, because bare-knuckle fighting had technically been made illegal in

America. Imagine the hype that Dana White would be able to build off that. (Incidentally, the match could be considered one of the first mixed martial arts fights, since, as documented by Mississippi Isshin-ryu Karate on its website, wrestling holds were permitted in the bout.)

In the end, the bout took place in Mississippi. It went an amazing 75 rounds before Kilrain's manager threw in the towel. Sullivan, who had only fought bare-knuckled on two previous occasions, was now the man who would go down in history as the last of his breed.

Perhaps it was because Sullivan racked up bouts both with and without gloves that Allen & Ginter's design team chose to depict Sullivan with his arms crossed over his hands. One would likely have expected Sullivan's fists to be cocked and ready to deal a blow in the classic boxer pose. Instead, it is a quiet, almost reflective Sullivan that we see on this card, one of the most beautiful produced in the A&G run.

More than a century after A&G cards first were collected, the brand was resurrected by Topps, which produced some of the most desirable and beautiful cards of the first decade of the 21st century. Staying true to the original series, Topps included sports stars from various disciplines in its set, including boxing. The initial set, released in 2006, featured Mike Tyson, a man who, like Sullivan, was considered among the elite of his era. One can only wonder what the result of a dream match between these two Allen & Ginter legends would be. ◀◀

Bart Starr

BACK – PACKERS

THE SAD TRUTH is that if you asked most people under the age of 35 today about Bart Starr, they'll probably sooner recall that he was part of a joke on *The Simpsons*, rather than his heroics on the football field. Complain about "kids these days" if you like, but almost anyone from Generation Y forward thinks the greatest Green Bay Packer quarterback of all time is Brett Favre — not Starr, the original gunslinger of the frozen tundra. Yet Bart arguably had a better career than Brett.

Starr debuted in 1957, the same year Johnny Unitas first hit the gridiron. His road to glory, though, wasn't a sure thing. Starr didn't assume the Green Bay starting job until 1959, but was a consummate professional who could manipulate a game and make his teammates work for him. His mastery was formidable as he guided the Packers to the first two Super Bowl titles and was named the game's MVP both times in the process. His performance in those two games was virtually a reprise of how he led the Packers to NFL championships in 1961 and 1962, prior to the league's merger with the AFL and the creation of the largest North American sporting event. Starr also led the Packers to an NFL championship in 1965.

Along with these championships, Starr also garnered NFL MVP honors in 1966, was named to two First Team and two Second Team NFL All-Pro squads, was named to the 1960s All-Decade team, was honored in the NFL and Green Bay Packer Halls of Fame and had his number retired.

It's hard to believe that he wasn't drafted until round 17 and

200th overall, yet that was the case when Green Bay plucked him after he'd finished his college career in Alabama. By the time that Starr had retired, he was an absolute marvel recognized as one of the NFL's elite performers and one of its most popular players off the field as well.

It is not surprising, then, that Starr has maintained a cult following among collectors who remember his glory days. Chief on their want lists is this rookie card which, like the Unitas, has become a legendary piece. The dual photo, albeit in separate boxes, would be something that Topps would use several times over in football and for various other sports, all the way through the modern era of trading cards.

Though the saga of the Topps/Fleer/Philadelphia adjustments between AFL and NFL contracts were still a few years away, the New York–based Topps had, at this point, solidified its position in pigskin picture cards, and its two rivals would immerse themselves in football collecting culture in the 1960s and become names as important as those of the legends of the gridiron. Unfortunately, Philadelphia wasn't long for the card world and can now only be found in brand revivals. Fleer would suffer a similar fate; the brand is now held by the Upper Deck Company. ◄◄

Jan. 23, 1959 — Ted Signs For 1959

IN THE LATE 1950s, the baseball card market was dominated by Topps. They sold millions of cards to American youth along with slabs of gum that are both beloved and reviled, depending on the opinion of the collector. However, a rival gum company based out of Philadelphia was about to become a thorn in their side with their first baseball card effort.

At the time, there were few veteran players more popular than Ted Williams of the Boston Red Sox, and while Topps had him sewn up into a contract that helped deal a death blow to Bowman a few years earlier, they were not prepared for another company to come in and scoop up the talented slugger for themselves. It was standard practice for Topps to offer a player $100 a year for the right to place him on a baseball card but Williams had a deal that commanded more money for the exclusive right to use his likeness.

Williams's deal with Topps expired in 1959, and when Fleer offered him an exorbitant sum, Topps simply would not match the offer. As a result, an 80-card collection showing highlights from the life of the Splendid Splinter hit store shelves. It was a revolutionary concept for the time as there had only been small regional or food issues that paid tribute to a single player. Kids could now get cards of Williams playing baseball along with a quirky shot of him posed with a giant marlin he caught while fishing in Peru.

However, a problem arose that had an impact on the production of the landmark set. Card number 68, simply entitled "Ted

Signs for '59," featured Williams signing a contract with Red Sox general manager Bucky Harris. Such a seemingly innocuous card would not normally generate much notice, but Harris was apparently under contract to Topps at the time. Fleer had to pull it from production, and as a result, the card became an instant rarity sought after by collectors ever since.

Another problem with this card is counterfeit copies. Fakes began to surface at card shows in the early 1970s, and since then, collectors finishing their sets have been forced to do their homework to avoid being ripped off.

The set proved to be a strong seller for Fleer, and it allowed the company to move further into the market. Over subsequent years, they produced three sets featuring baseball greats and then attempted a collection of active players in 1963, which included a small, horrible-tasting cherry cookie instead of gum since Topps had a monopoly on that idea. Ultimately, Fleer would launch a major legal challenge that ultimately opened up the market and put all manufacturers on an equal playing field. But that would not take place until 1980, and for many years, Topps essentially had the market to themselves. ◀ ◀

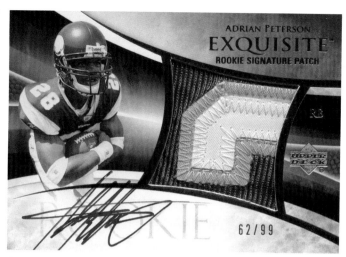

THE TURN- around in football cards has been nothing short of phenomenal. The sport with the shortest season but most dedicated fanbase has often seemed to lag behind others in collectibles.

In recent history, it's arguably attributable to a lack of dominating rookies. Until Peyton Manning stepped onto the scene in 1998, football was ruled by players whose performances were fantastic but were for the most part isolated to only a few teams. Ask anyone who the top names from the gridiron were in the late '80s and early '90s, and they'll probably pick a San Fransisco 49er (Steve Young, Joe Montana or Jerry Rice), a Dallas Cowboy (Troy Aikman or Emmitt Smith) and a Green Bay Packer (Brett Favre or Reggie White). Maybe they'll pick Miami's Dan Marino or Denver's John Elway.

And really, that was it. Promises of greatness from new draft picks quickly fell short of expectations. First-overall picks like Ki-Jana Carter (Cincinnati) and Steve Emtman (Indianapolis) didn't excite collectors. Many other players would either sit on the sidelines for a couple years and collect dust (not the recipe for instant gratification that collectors desired) or would be a bust upon their debut. Thus, the most regionalized of all sports found itself without draws in every city. When you don't have a superstar, your card market can suffer, and if your city hated one of the top-drawing teams, you weren't going to sell a lot of product.

Then, Carson Palmer, Ben Roethlisberger and others really started to open up a new trend. Not only did such players make immediate impacts in the league, but they were stars for teams that had either been mediocre or bottom-dwellers. Suddenly, collectors in those markets stood up and took notice, as did the general collecting community. If a collector didn't like the Chargers' Philip Rivers, for example, they had Cardinals wunderkind Larry Fitzgerald to pursue.

Among these new stars was one of the most exciting running backs ever to enter the league — Adrian Peterson. A.D. (short for All-Day, a nickname he's had since he was a toddler), a recruit out of the heart of Sooner country, was already something of a household name when he was taken seventh overall by the Minnesota Vikings. A collarbone injury may have caused other teams to shy away from him in the draft, but they would end up paying the price. Peterson captured offensive Rookie of the Year honors and served notice that every rushing record was in jeopardy when he broke the mark for most running yards in a single game.

Anticipation for A-Pete's arrival into the card market was unbelievable even before he stepped foot on the field, so you can imagine the excitement as card after card was pulled from new sets, each one more precious than the last. Minnesota collectors soon forgot the bitter sting that accompanied Randy Moss's departure a couple years prior. And just as it had done with LeBron James a few years earlier, Upper Deck issued an Exquisite Collection card containing both a Peterson patch and autograph in an edition serial-numbered to 99 copies.

It was like the 2003–04 NBA season all over again, and Peterson's most valuable RC was surrounded by other attention grabbers, including Marshawn Lynch and Calvin Johnson.

Since his first year in the league, Peterson has maintained his standing of being the best rusher of his generation. He is a three-time First Team All-Pro, has competed in three Pro Bowls and is a constant threat to break open any game.

And just like other NFL stars across the country, Peterson has not only been a regional star, but has become a superstar the league can hang its hat on during one of its most successful eras. ◀ ◀

OH FOR THE DAYS WHEN Brett Favre was not retiring . . . every season.

Believe it or not, there was a time when the man who would become one of the best passers of his generation was not spending each offseason at a press conference, in tears, talking about how much the game of football meant to him and how much he would miss it. No, at the time of this card's release, young Favre was more concerned about his future in the game than his future away from it.

Favre had yet to join the Green Bay Packers when he was photographed for this card, part of what was one of the first premium sets in sports. Stadium Club was, at the time, one of the most expensively packed card sets across all the big four sports. There was good reason for the premium on these cards though — as indicated on the wrapping, the cards feature Kodak quality photography!

Okay, so the Kodak logo probably didn't do a lot to sell packs, but there's no denying that Stadium Club has, year in and year out, produced some of the most amazing pictures ever to be found on cardboard. With minimalist designs, some cards stand out as art, worthy of display rather than being kept hidden away in a box or binder.

Stadium Club also benefited from multiple release formats. While the basic series was issued in the standard pack form,

Topps took this brand in different directions, including creating a special series just for its collector club (Charter Member, later known as Members Only, series) and releasing updated series in either boxed sets or in miniature replica casings from, for example, the 1991 MLB All-Star Game in Toronto.

But of all the cards created across the four sports, especially in the first Stadium Club season, it is the Favre that stands tall.

At the time, Favre was, shall we say, "unimpressive" as a rookie with the Atlanta Falcons. After throwing an interception with his very first pass, Favre floundered, going 0–4 on tosses and adding a second interception. It's not necessarily his fault that his career started so horribly — management wasn't exactly encouraging. As *Milwaukee Journal Sentinel* scribe Tom Silverstein wrote in a September 24, 2005, tribute article, Coach Jerry Glanville once said that it would take a plane crash for Favre to get into a game.

It wasn't until he moved to Green Bay that Favre began to shine. With a solid receiving corps and strong line in front of him, he would become one of the most prolific passers in NFL history, leading the Packers to victory in two Super Bowls. Favre would also establish a new Iron Horse record for QBs, not missing a start for an astounding 297 straight games. A Sunday break was never in the cards for Favre, even amidst tragic events such as his father's passing.

Despite the wealth of memorabilia devoted to Favre, very little commemorates his pre-Packer days. Perhaps it's due to a lack of interest, but very few cards picture Brett in college or as a Falcon. ◀ ◀

FOR A TIME, THE 1980 TOPPS Rickey Henderson was a must-have for collectors, especially when he was in the midst of trying to become Major League Baseball's all-time leader in stolen bases. To this day it remains one of the most popular cards of its era.

A colorful and sometimes controversial character, Henderson was one of the top names in baseball and widely collected. In 1982, he would set an incredible standard by swiping 130 bases in a single season. After beginning his career with the Oakland Athletics, he joined the New York Yankees in 1985 and he was able to get incredible public exposure in a major media center. In 1989, he would return to Oakland and help his team to a World Series title, earning Most Valuable Player of the American League Championship Series.

In 1990, Henderson was arguably at his peak when he finished second among all American League players with a .325 batting average and earned regular season MVP honors as well. Baseball card collectors and investors embraced all his cards, but his highly prized rookie card from the 1980 Topps set was the one to get. If that wasn't enough, the card got another major boost when he broke Lou Brock's record for most career stolen bases on May 1, 1991. For the next few years, the card continued to be popular as he continued to perform at the big league level, but like most cards popular in the early 1990s, there's been an inevitable decline in its value.

Despite his induction into the Baseball Hall of Fame, the demand for Henderson's card has softened. There are fewer baseball collectors today, in general, and those with interest in the card probably already have it. This isn't a reflection on Henderson, rather it's more of an indication of the direction the hobby took. Still, the tail-end of Henderson's career certainly didn't help matters; bouncing from team to team and from league to league in an attempt to resurrect his former glory wasn't good for his hobby value.

The original negative for the photograph used on the rookie card went up for auction in 2009 by the Topps Vault and sold for $821 — to the surprise of many hobby observers. ◀ ◀

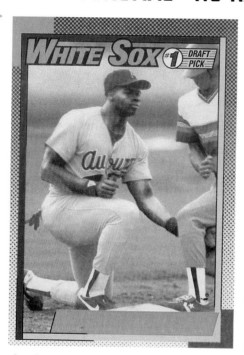

FOR A TIME THE "NO NAME" version of the 1990 Topps Frank Thomas card was one of the hottest items in the hobby. Its origins are shrouded in mystery, and people have different theories about how it came into existence.

In 1990, Topps put out one of its most colorful issues ever. The design has seen its fair share of criticism from collectors over the years, and to its further detriment, it's also part of the overproduction era and lacks high-dollar RCs. As a result, it's rarely considered a must-have unless someone is working on a run of complete sets. It may gain support over the next few years, like the oft-maligned 1975 design, but without any major rookies, it's going to be a long climb to respectability.

However, there are a couple of 1990 cards that were leaked out in wax packs that may have some busting packs in the hopes of finding a major hit. The first is a card featuring then President of the United States George Bush in the baseball uniform he wore when he played for Yale University. According to a magazine issued by Topps at the time, the card was produced when Bush's grandson asked why his grandfather never had a baseball card. When Topps heard about this, a small quantity were produced and given to the Bush family. Some of these cards leaked out over the years and there were reports of some appearing in packs. Still a high-dollar item due to incredible scarcity, the Bush card rarely comes up for sale and may not be in the best condition. Nobody seems to care, though, since it's one of the most unusual cards of the era.

A printing error created the Thomas card, and for some strange reason it did not immediately surface as something for variation hunters to chase. It wasn't until Thomas arrived as a superstar that his cards truly took off, spurred by another release — his 1990 Leaf rookie card that appeared in Series 2 packs. The first premium baseball card set, the "Leaf Set" was produced by Donruss in limited (for the time) quantities and featured the first use of metallic ink on a baseball card.

For a time, it was the hobby's hottest set, but the discovery of the "No Name" card made a new king among Thomas's rookie issues.

The regular card in the base set has Thomas in his collegiate uniform as part of a subset that features some of the top picks in the 1989 MLB draft. However, a savvy collector discovered that one of his cards was missing the player's name. For many years, error cards had been one of the hottest items around, but they had cooled significantly by the time the Thomas was reported to the hobby media. According to research done by collectors, packs containing the "No Name" were distributed in the New England area but no one knows how many copies of the Thomas exist.

There are a number of theories about how the error occurred, but the most accepted and logical theory is that it's the result of black ink missing from a portion of the card due to a bad printing plate or negative. On the printed sheet, several of the neighboring cards also show some color degradation due to ink being blocked from reaching the printing surface. This creates some more interesting variations to chase down, but the major hobby publications have yet to recognize their existence.

Thomas spent the rest of the 1990s as one of the most collectible players on the market, and he would go on to hit over 500 career home runs. Once he is enshrined in the Baseball Hall of Fame, there may be renewed interest in the "No Name" card, but it will always be considered one of the hobby's greatest variations. ◀ ◀

NO MATTER THE ERA, A STAR'S first card, in virtually every case, has carried a sizable premium.

When a player's card pictures him next to the elite veterans of his sport, it suggests that he belongs among their ranks. Often these cards will be found in special subsets with enticing names like "Super Rookie" or "Young Guns." The sets will often consist of a good number of players who either have a couple games under their belts or have been standouts in college or junior leagues across North America (and sometimes overseas).

But when a company dedicates a subset to one single player, the natural collector inclination is to feel that this player is something special, and no one will deny that feeling was present when Eric Lindros was formally introduced to the hockey world via the Future Superstar title in Score's first hockey set.

Lindros, then of the Oshawa Generals, was already gaining a reputation as being "The Next One," when an upstart company that had already had a measure of success in baseball and football brought the player into the hobby spotlight. It didn't take much effort for the youngster to get a lot of hype, having already received some good pickup on his 7th Inning Sketch junior cards.

The key to the Lindros card was that Score had secured an exclusive contract with him, the first of its kind in hockey. The regular Score series card, both its American and its perceived-as-more-rare Canadian version, were soon joined by cards in the Rookie and Traded and Young Superstars series, as well as a group of five "bonus" cards of Eric that were inserted into factory sets.

Despite his exclusive contract, Lindros was also featured in the inaugural Upper Deck series in 1990–91, which included stars of Canada's World Junior squad. Score's exclusive deal was able to prevent UD from featuring "The Next One" individually, but it did not, as it turned out, prevent the California-based company from producing "Canada's Captains," which featured Lindros, Kris Draper and Stephen Rice together on a card.

Of all the Lindros cards produced, however, the Score remains the most popular. For years, up until the emergence of Martin Brodeur, Lindros's was the most valuable card Score produced that year, and the most valuable card *not* produced that year by O-Pee-Chee or Pro Set (yes, you read that right).

Lindros's career, however, did not live up to the hype. While he was a solid performer, The Big E sustained multiple concussions and a variety of other ailments. He'd win one Hart Memorial Trophy as league MVP and would reach the Stanley Cup finals with Philadelphia, but Lindros would not attain any significant records. Despite this, he remains one of the most prominent players in hobby history. Lindros was the ultimate prospect in the card market's boom era, and for that reason alone his rookie card remains one of the most desired cards of all time (even if you can now find it in the dollar bin at a local card show). There may have been no better indicator of this continued lust for Lindros's RC than when Panini issued buyback autographs of the card in its 2010–11 series. One of the first Lindros cards to appear on eBay's auction block ended up selling for more than $2,000. ◀ ◀

IT'S AMAZING THE DIFFERENCE a year can make — in a player's development and in how he can sway fan approval. Case in point: Alexander Ovechkin. In 2005, in Canada, Ovechkin was public enemy number one. His cocky attitude at the World Junior Hockey Championships, playing for Russia, rubbed a lot of fans the wrong way. He was boastful, brash and, most importantly, a threat to Canada's dominance and its team led by its own junior sensation, Sidney Crosby.

Less than a year later though, OV, as he would come to be known, was the toast of the NHL. Though Crosby was knighted the league's premier superstar and the new face of hockey, Ovechkin showed that he wasn't going to let Sid the Kid hog the spotlight. Ovechkin put on highlight reel performances virtually every time he stepped on the ice, scoring goals in the most unbelievable fashions. Many pundits called a goal he scored against the Phoenix Coyotes that season the greatest ever scored, thanks to his masterful acrobatics and ability to concentrate.

Following that campaign, OV not only became a fan favorite, but hardcore followers and media-ites alike were ready to anoint him, and not Crosby, as the league's new prodigy. Ovechkin captured the Calder Trophy over El Sid in what some considered a surprising victory.

The hobby, however, reacted differently. Crosby was already

a familiar and, indeed, hot commodity by the time he stepped foot on NHL ice, thanks to a number of products by In The Game, Inc., including his own series. Though Ovechkin was far from being an afterthought, his celebrity wasn't quite as well established.

That was the situation when both young men entered the NHL and were eligible for their rookie cards. Crosby was the centerpiece of Upper Deck's Series One release, while Ovechkin was saved for the second series (one that featured a devoted Crosby insert set). Crosby also had a boxed set produced by UD; OV did not.

The demand for the two stars was equally as one-sided. Book values and trade board demands were much higher for Sid the Kid than Alexander the Gr8. Despite OV's superior rookie season, by the time the 2006 NHL Entry Draft took place, Ovechkin was playing a distant second fiddle, defying most statutes of hobby logic — except for one. . . .

Despite the fact that NHL brass, teams and fans like to describe hockey as the sport that has the greatest international following, there's a cloud that hangs over its hobby base. For whatever reason, be it national pride or something else, stars born and trained in countries other than the epicenter of its collecting universe — Canada — have not gained the measure of popularity of homegrown stars. Whether it was Martin Brodeur gaining more of the spotlight than Dominik Hašek, or Jaromir Jagr playing second fiddle to Joe Sakic, foreign-born superstars have not been able to match up dollar for hobby dollar against their Canadian-born counterparts.

Ovechkin has started to buck that trend. He ranks as one of the most popular players in the hobby, and his The Cup rookie is a fine example of this. Limited to 99 copies (similar to the Exquisite-branded cards of LeBron James and Adrian Peterson), these cards rarely appear for sale, and when they do (provided they're legitimate and the patch swatches haven't been swapped), they command big bucks — into four digits.

With a bright future ahead, it's possibile that Ovechkin will become one of the all-time hobby elites. ◀ ◀

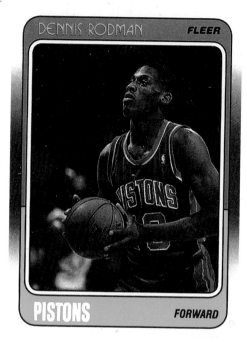

IT WAS HARD TO PICK ONLY ONE card from 1987–88 Fleer Basketball release for this book. Arguably one of the most significant sets of the 1980s, it was loaded with rookies, including Scottie Pippen and John Stockton. The members of the holy trinity of '80s basketball (Michael Jordan, Larry Bird and Magic Johnson) were still in their prime and attracting collectors. Furthermore, the set was typical of Fleer's NBA entries, utilizing All-Star stickers that helped entice kids to purchase packages, much as the logo stickers in baseball did.

But of all the cards that came out of packs that year, none holds an audience today like the Dennis Rodman. Affectionately known as The Worm, Rodman was, and continues to be, a pioneer in the world of sport. Perhaps better than any other athlete, he was able to combine athletics with theatrics, and the result was a reputation of unpredictability that drew fans and detractors alike to watch his every move — one week, Rodman might have green hair, the next he'd be promoting a book wearing a wedding dress, then, a week later, he was married to Carmen Electra.

All of this would not matter, however, if Rodman couldn't get it done on the court. Rodman was one of the best rebounders of his era. His first team, the Detroit Pistons, was one of the most popular crews of the decade, with Isiah Thomas leading the way. Rodman would later join the Chicago Bulls and, with

Jordan, Pippen and other fantastic players, capture three NBA championships to go along with two titles he earned with the Pistons. Rodman was a two-time Defensive Player of the Year and multi-time All-Defensive First Team member. His career, which also included stints with the San Antonio Spurs, Los Angeles Lakers and Dallas Mavericks, certainly has the makings of a Hall of Fame induction.

But what detracts from Rodman's status, however, is powerful. His stellar career was marred by his reputation as as selfish player. Practices, preseason, even regular league games weren't a priority when other opportunities, such as getting huge paydays from World Championship Wrestling, were presented. He would also be fined and suspended for on-court rule violations such as headbutting Stacey King. These things severely impacted his popularity, both with fans and in the memorabilia market.

The result of all this drama has been that Rodman's RC has gone up and down in value, depending on whether fans are happy with him or sick of his latest shtick. Regardless, "Rodzilla's" first card preserves a player who was, at one time, as clean-cut as they came. ◄ ◄

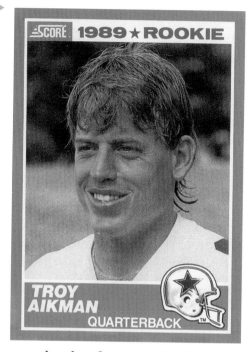

IN THE EARLY 1990s, FOOT-ball was dominated by two teams — one was the Buffalo Bills, who reached new levels of ineptitude by going oh-for-four straight Super Bowls. Two of those losses came against the other gridiron kings — America's Team, the Dallas Cowboys.

The Boys were led by a trio known as The Triplets. During an amazing run of three Superbowl titles in four years, receiver Michael Irvin, running back Emmitt Smith and quarterback Troy Aikman were the stars. And while Irvin and Smith are undeniably two of the greatest players in Dallas history, it's Aikman most collectors turn to when discussing football supremacy.

No one will ever question that Troy Aikman is among the greatest QBs of the 1990s. His stats do all the talking: six-straight Pro Bowls, one NFL Man of the Year award, one Superbowl MVP, a career 81.6 passer rating and a 61.5 completion percentage. He would, of course, earn his spot in the Hall of Fame and in Dallas's famed Ring of Honor alongside the likes of Roger Staubach and Don Meredith.

Like many athletes, Aikman has also been able to keep his name in the spotlight. Today, he's one of Fox's lead broadcasters. Because of this, a generation of fans who did not see him play can hear his calls as he draws on a wealth of experience to analyze the gridiron wars. Maintaining his public profile has definitely helped ensure a following for his cards, and the most popular among them is the Score offering pictured here.

Breaking Topps's long-standing pigskin dominance, Score introduced a new type of card in 1989 — one that looked and felt different. Even their packaging was new: the standard wax wrappers replaced with a rubbery plastic encasement.

Collectors embraced the new product in a big way, favoring Score over the competition, especially the Pro Set counterpart, which featured Aikman in college action. The Score card was one of the first opportunities to get Aikman in the white and blue.

Though the design of this card might be considered simple, it has a certain elegance. It was classy enough to inspire Score to bring it back in 2009, though by this time the company was owned by Panini. By the end of the first decade of the 2000s, Aikman's RC had established itself as one of football's greatest, as had several other cards produced by Score in the years before the company went south in the early 1990s and became inundated with the problems that would plague it for the remainder of its existence. ◀ ◀

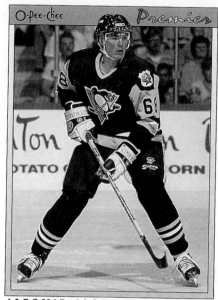

JAROMIR JAGR
PENGUINS • RIGHT WING/AILIER DROIT

IF THERE WAS A SINGLE season that marked everything changing for hockey card collectors, it was 1990–91. The NHL and the NHLPA offered licensing to more than one trading card manufacturer and the old standbys, O-Pee-Chee and Topps, needed to come up with something quick in order to compete against the three-headed monster that was Pro Set, Score and Upper Deck.

For Topps, it was pretty much business as usual. They put out their largest base card set ever and also released hockey cards under their revitalized Bowman brand. Since O-Pee-Chee lived and died with hockey, it followed up its annual effort with the release of O-Pee-Chee Premier — the hobby's first premium set of hockey trading cards. With metallic inks, players on their new teams, superstars and rookies, it came out of the gate slowly but proved to be the year's most popular and enduring release.

As the buzz built, dealers and collectors who didn't hop on the Premier bandwagon from the start quickly scrambled to try to get their hands on packs and boxes. Complete sets jumped in price almost daily and singles were a hot commodity. A second wave of boxes surfaced and factory sets were issued, but it still wasn't enough to keep up with demand.

It is especially interesting that Premier was printed on the brilliant white Tembec stock that O-Pee-Chee had tested the previous year for a short one-sheet run of their regular set. This short run later made its way into the hands of collectors and is sought-after today due to its scarcity. The paper was used for the regular 1990–91 set and proved versatile enough for the Premier cards.

Jaromir Jagr was a fresh-faced rookie in 1990–91, and it was only natural that he would be a part of the 132-card set. At the time, collectors were more interested in the first card of Sergei Fedorov in a Detroit Red Wings uniform, but history would eventually make the Jagr the collection's top card. At one point, it was one of the hottest cards around, but as his hobby prestige decreased, it seemed that anyone who might want the card already had one.

As was the case with almost every set issued in the boom era, boxed sets of O-Pee-Chee Premier would make their way onto the market. Of course, back in the '90s, anyone who dared open a sealed set was devaluing it, even though there was no difference between a sealed card and a pack-pulled version. Eventually, collectors caught on and the boxed sets were busted and the Jagrs, Fedorovs and other rookies plucked and sold.

Jagr would become one of the sport's top stars and he would earn a number of accolades before heading overseas in 2008 to play in the Kontinental Hockey League. The demand for his O-Pee-Chee Premier rookie card would subside, but there is no denying how important the set was at the peak of the boom years. Quite affordable today, it is a wonderful reminder of how hype can inflate a card's value and how much the collecting world has changed. ◄ ◄

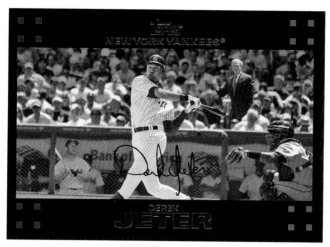

WHEN YOU MAKE a list like this, whether it's composed of the best ever or something as simple as a group of highlights, you're tempted to throw in something a little fun. . . . And we've given in to that instinct by including this Derek Jeter card.

Back in 2007, Topps was looking to shake things up a bit. At that point, base cards had pretty much become the ugly stepsister in the happy little home known as a card pack. Compared with the gorgeous jersey and autograph cards, they lacked pizzazz. Some collectors would even go so far as to leave these pieces in hobby shops after busting a box.

To buck the trend Topps created a variation of its standard Jeter card. Rather than the vertical card, showing the Yankee marquee star making a fielding play, the horizontal version shows Jeter completing his swing as Mickey Mantle looks on from the dugout and then U.S. President George W. Bush cheers from the stands.

Yes, you read that right.

The card, unannounced at first, soon became one of the most in-demand in recent memory. eBay sales were volatile and message boards were cluttered with demand as a pack of hungry wolves clamored to devour this unique card.

The story behind its creation varied as the card hit the mainstream media. At first, Topps was shy about it, attributing the Photoshop wizardry to an office prankster. Later, the truth was revealed: the card was indeed a planned insert. As Topps spokesman Clay Luraschi told ESPN, the card was created by the company's creative department and was in fact approved before it was packed out.

"We encourage our creative department to be as creative as possible," Luraschi told reporter David Schoetz for a February 27, 2007, article. "They had a sense of humor to do something like this. We thought it was funny." Funny enough to spawn a few other cards that would play off the theme.

One year later, football got its taste of Topps's photo gimmickry, and this time fun came with Brett Favre. The Green Bay Packers quarterback had announced his retirement and seemed done with the game. The boys and girls in New York responded by creating two variants of what could have been the final Favre card from Topps — one with a ghosted image of the late, great Vince Lombardi, and the other of "Favre" sitting on a riding mower.

Brett would almost have the last laugh, however, as he came out of retirement to play for the New York Jets — *almost*, because Topps followed Favre to the Big Apple, putting the lawnmower in Times Square.

Though the Jeter card's appeal has softened somewhat, it stands out as one of the greatest intentional variants in baseball card history — just as the player will go down as this generation's greatest Yankee. ◀◀◀

PLAYERS THAT BREAK LONG- standing barriers in sports are often remembered by fans for their bravery and dedication to their game, and the growing fanbase for women's hockey looks to Manon Rhéaume as a true pioneer because she first broke the gender barrier at the pro level.

On November 26, 1991, Rhéaume got an opportunity to suit up for the Trois-Rivières Draveurs of the Quebec Major Junior Hockey League and caused a media sensation in Canada. When she appeared in 17 minutes of action in a loss to the Granby Bisons, she managed to catch the attention of the NHL's Tampa Bay Lightning — a club looking to make a splash heading into its first season in the league. Rhéaume would see limited action in an exhibition game against the St. Louis Blues. While it was later admitted by Tampa Bay General Manager Phil Esposito that it was a publicity stunt, she would earn a spot with their farm team, the Atlanta Knights of the International Hockey League.

With all of the hype surrounding her groundbreaking achievement, Classic Games made sure that she would be included in their upcoming 1992 Hockey Draft Picks set featuring some of the game's hottest young prospects. It proved to be a smart move as the product sold in massive quantities, mostly for the shot at pulling Rhéaume's first trading card from a pack.

Naturally, Classic maximized their use of Rhéaume over the

course of three seasons and produced a wide variety of cards ranging from base cards to autographs and inserts. If there was an opportunity to include the young goalie in a product, they were going to do it, and as a result, she became overexposed in the market. At times, it became somewhat ridiculous, like with the curious case of the 1993 Pro Prospects collection that had eight cards of Rhéaume in a set of 150 players. Then again, that was often the nature of the industry at the time, as manufacturers wanted to make the most off their investment in a player.

On the other hand, Classic did make a shrewd move in 1994 by building on the goodwill generated by Rhéaume and putting together the Women of Hockey insert set featuring both Canadian and American women's players that played in the 1994 World Championship tournament. As a result, collectors had a chance to obtain the first cards of stars such as Cassie Campbell and Hayley Wickenheiser. At this point, Rhéaume's hobby popularity had died down, as has the demand for her card.

She was not done racking up the accolades, though, and she was a part of Canada's silver medal–winning team at the 1998 Winter Games in Nagano, Japan. After her retirement from the game, her name is still spoken of with high regard as she inspired countless young girls to take up hockey as a sport. Today, her cards are relatively affordable and adding a base card or autograph to a collection serves as a reminder that gender should not limit a player's ambitions. ◀ ◀

EPILOGUE

SPORTS CARDS AREN'T for kids any more.

No matter how the leagues try to spin it, the idea of a child going down to the corner store to break open a pack of cards is an antiquated notion. Kids were driven out of the hobby more than 15 years ago and very few youngsters embrace the tradition today. With the online world, video games and a multitude of other diversions, you really can't blame them, either.

Some collectors and dealers put a lot of effort into bringing youth back to the hobby, but when it started to become an adult's game in the 1980s it became another beast entirely. Now, greed often drives the hobby, and what was once a quaint pastime has became something that raises more eyebrows than excitement from the public. For some, dealers and collectors have been reduced to stereotypes and changing that perception lies squarely in the hands of those who remain in the hobby today.

Once in a while, the industry gets a little bit of mainstream media attention and a good portion of the publicity can be negative. In a recent example, a Michigan-based accountant named Robert J. Power paid an incredible $16,403 for a card of pitching prospect Stephen Strasburg. The 2010 Bowman Superfractor (an amped-up version of the rainbow-foiled Refractor) was only limited to one copy, and the hype surrounding Strasburg drove the price of the card to an unreal level. Pressured by a number of sources to sell the card, Power put it up for auction once again and he made $5,000 on the deal, despite the fact that when he sent it in to Beckett to be graded it was assigned a 9.5 rating for poor centering. Not a bad profit, but the news stories surrounding the card tended to focus on the financial aspect of things rather than examining the state of the hobby.

Did the hype bring some collectors back? Possibly, but there is a greater chance that they will be the fly-by-night investors who helped alter the hobby in the early 1990s instead of those who appreciate card collecting for what it really is. Soon after, Strasburg was forced onto the disabled list for the dreaded "Tommy John surgery." He's not expected to return to action until 2012. In the meantime, the value of his other cards is certain to soften and it may be a good time to pick some up to make a profit once he returns. As of September 2010, his cards are still in demand — but certainly not at the level they were prior to his injury.

As time passes, the hobby will see more heavily hyped prospects, and as always, the rookie card will drive the industry. Bryce Harper, for example, was already being touted as the "next big thing" in cards — just a scant few weeks after the Strasburg phenomenon began petering out.

Manufacturers have also faced problems recently, as the major sports leagues award exclusive licenses or attempt to keep certain companies out of the picture. Competition creates choice for the consumer and will also hopefully foster industry growth. Sales aren't anywhere near where they were 15 or 20 years ago, and companies have to be more creative and offer greater value in their products with each passing year. Also, manufacturers need to be responsible to the industry and not shatter the trust they have established with collectors. For the past few years, Upper Deck has suffered through a public relations nightmare: the once seemingly untouchable company has lost its NFL, NBA and MLB licenses. It's something that they may never be able to recover from, and it has already had a major impact on dealers whose doors stayed open because of the Upper Deck releases that were coming out on what was once a weekly basis. If Upper Deck fades away, you can bet that a lot of card stores will be out of business as well.

If the general public really becomes interested in trading cards again, it will lead to good times — for manufacturers, dealers and collectors. However, let's hope we can learn from the mistakes of the early 1990s and create a hobby that is fun for all, rather than dominated by the almighty dollar. ◀ ◀

NOTES ON THE PHOTOS

THANK YOU TO ALL WHO contributed to this project, including:

In The Game Inc., Panini America Inc., The Topps Company Inc. and The Upper Deck Company for permission to use images of their cards, images and background photography.

Joe Orlando, president of Professional Sport Authenticators, for supplying the vast majority of our sports card images.

Beckett Media LLC, Robert Edward Auctions, Dave and Adam's Card World (Buffalo, NY), Burbank Sports Cards (Burbank, CA), Mill Creek Sports (Seattle, WA), baseball-cards.com, Jim and Steve's Sportscards (Waukegan, IL), Ryan Cracknell of Trader Crack's, Patrick Greenough of radicards.com, Ryan Hank of The Miracle Shop, Robert Nona Jr., Trevor Patterson, Daniel Poor, Andy Malycky, Jeff Griffin, Rich Treonze, Jeremy Lee, Ronnie Tomberlin, Mike Fermaglich, and eBay sellers Bori11 and bertg71 for providing other card images.

Beckett Grading Services, Superstars Sportcards and Collectibles (Winnipeg, MB), the organizers of the Toronto Sportcard and Memorabilia Expo and vendors at the Expo and shows in Winnipeg for providing additional images. ◀◀